100

THINGS TO DO IN
WICHITA
BEFORE YOU
DIE

VANESSA WHITESIDE

REEDY PRESS

Library of Congress Control Number: 2021950829

ISBN: 9781681063577

Design by Jill Halpin

All photos by the author unless otherwise noted.

Printed in the United States of America
22 23 24 25 26   5 4 3 2 1

100

THINGS TO DO IN
WICHITA
BEFORE YOU
DIE

Jake &
Tessa —
Such a pleasure to
meet you!

Vanessa Whiteside

#staycurious

DEDICATION

For my fellow Wichitans, who inspired me to write a book about the amazing place we get to call home.

For Mom, who chose Wichita, and for Chris, who is always ready for an adventure.

• •

CONTENTS

Music and Entertainment

Culture and History

Shopping and Fashion

PREFACE

When I was in my teens, I took Wichita for granted and wanted to move away. One day I did, but like many residents, I moved back. I was better for it. Because what I was looking for in a city was here the whole time. Genuine people. Entertaining things to do. Affordable living.

I didn't just fall in love with Wichita, I fell head over heels for it. Soon, I found myself telling others about hidden-away neighborhood restaurants. Enthusiastically informing friends about unforgettable concert experiences. Recounting the sounds and excitement of festivals and sporting events.

With so much to do in one city, I needed to create a bucket list of places to visit so I could check them off one by one, a challenging endeavor. Limiting my list to 100 experiences was a daunting task. A native Wichitan, I trusted my gut, but I also asked others for their recommendations. "What if someone had never been to Wichita before?" I asked myself. "What if they've lived here all their life but yearn to discover new places?" I revisited tried-and-true locations and hidden gems. I dined out. I drove to every part of town. While there are more than enough things to do within the city limits, I finally composed a list that represents the quintessential things to do in Wichita.

I hope that this guidebook inspires you to discover destinations unknown and well-known. Dog-ear the pages and write notes in the margins. Better yet, throw it in your car and use it as a resource, like a *Choose Your Own Adventure®* book.

Ultimately, I want you to love Wichita as much as I do. Because all we ever wanted in a city is right here, waiting to be discovered.

Stay curious.

ACKNOWLEDGMENTS

First and foremost, I want to thank Jessica Sawatski for recommending me to Reedy Press. To the museum employees, restaurant workers, retail store owners, and everyone who took a little extra time to help me with the research of this book, thank you. You shared your time and your knowledge, and for that, I'm most grateful.

FOOD AND DRINK

ENJOY A SLICE OF HEAVEN
AT PEACE LOVE & PIE

Remember the pie your grandma made? You can find it at Peace Love & Pie, a shop located within steps of Naftzger Park in downtown Wichita. The buttery crust and gooey center of All American Apple or Chocolate Peanut Butter Mousse await your tastebuds. Take it to the next level by topping a slice with à la mode. If you're feeling non-traditional, try an AppPieTizer like the shop's popular Cinnamon Pie Fries, dipped in vanilla sauce.

Decadent? Yes. But as they say, "Life is a Pie Away," and it's worth every bite. Share your love of pastry with others by ordering a whole pie, which is available with a gluten-free butter crust. When you don't want to bake your own pie, buy a pie kit outfitted with instructions and ingredients for at-home baking.

645 E Douglas Ave., Ste. 104, 316-440-4706
andpie.shop

TIP
Naftzger Park, near the shop, is a busy location. Don't fret. Drivers can park behind the building for free Monday-Friday after 5 p.m. It's open anytime on weekends.

MUNCH ON A MEATY SANDWICH
AT NuWAY

"Crumbly is better!®" NuWAY has served loose meat sandwiches, fresh-made onion rings, and homemade root beer in Wichita to diehard fans since 1930. The original building on Douglas Avenue remains in operation in the historic Delano District. It is a popular hangout for regulars and out-of-towners, who drive for miles to curb their cravings. For good reason. If you're a regular, the staff often remembers your order.

While some purists prefer the classic sandwich with mustard, onion, and pickle, others choose the deluxe version with cheese. Children love the kids' meal that comes with root beer and ice cream. Stop by on Sundays to enjoy buy-one, get-one-free Junior NuWAYs with a purchase of a drink from the comfort of a retro booth or counter barstool.

1416 W Douglas Ave., 316-260-1131
7301 W Central Ave., 316-722-2217
6428 E Central Ave., 316-682-2261
3441 E Harry St., 316-684-6132
nuwayburgers.com

STUFF YOUR FACE
AT ZIGGY'S PIZZA

When you want to satisfy a craving for scratch-made pizza or sandwiches, the only place to pig out is Ziggy's Pizza. The family-owned business gets rave reviews from fans for its menu options served in a casual atmosphere.

Ziggy's likes to keep patrons guessing, using non-traditional ingredients. Flavorful toppings like mac and cheese, Nashville hot chicken, and cream cheese make appearances on pies. Ask about the Pizza of the Month. Passionate about sandwiches? Italian Toasty and Cluck Norris roll through a convection oven to melted perfection and don't disappoint.

All locations include patio dining, but date night is perfected when you walk to the Douglas Avenue location for dinner after strolling College Hill Park.

3700 E Douglas Ave., Ste. 100, 316-613-2529
8404 W 13th St. N, Ste. 100, 316-201-1811
12115 E 21st St. N, Ste. 105, 316-779-8181
ziggyswichita.com

LEAVE NO BITE BEHIND
AT BAGATELLE BAKERY

When the Toubia family opened Bagatelle Bakery in 1983, they gave the city a gift. From that year forward, Wichitans have loved their perfected European baked goods and lunch fare. On any given day, especially during lunch, the bakery and café see a steady stream of customers. People arrive wanting homemade empanadas, bierocks, or quiche. While some customers stop by to pick up a loaf of fresh-baked bread, others stay for a meal that never disappoints. Don't think of leaving without having dessert. One look inside the glass case and you'll want a pastry. Lovers of Bagatelle Bakery also adore their artistic cakes for special occasions.

6801 E Harry St., 316-684-5662
bagatellebakery.com

TIP
Do yourself a favor and buy grab-and-go items for tonight's dinner or tomorrow's lunch from the refrigerated case. Snag a bag of soft pita bread before heading to the register.

LICK THE BOWL CLEAN
AT TANYA'S SOUP KITCHEN

When you dine at Tanya's Soup Kitchen, you're going to have to shred every ounce of self-consciousness, because the desire to eat every crumb and lick the bowl clean is real.

Known for serving a rotating menu of soups, sandwiches, and salads using in-season ingredients, Tanya's Soup Kitchen's menu tempts your tastebuds, and diners can expect to devour their meals. Will you order the smoked red lentil soup? The Caprese BLT sandwich made with handcrafted pesto? No matter the choice, you'll want to order a second helping. Consider yourself warned: you'll crave dessert. Depending on the chef's whim, it may be a homemade cookie or bread pudding.

The line forms quickly at this popular lunch spot. Arrive early to find seating indoors or on the covered patio. Delicious food comes standard. Friendly customer service is a bonus.

1725 E Douglas Ave., Ste. 105, 316-267-7687
tskwichita.com

TIP
Craving soup at home? The restaurant has compiled some of its tastiest soup recipes onto recipe cards, which are for sale at the counter and on their website.

DINE IN A HISTORIC BUILDING
AT PUBLIC

Enjoy a delicious dinner in what used to be the Wichita Casket Company Building, built in 1916. Since 2012, the Public has used sustainable ingredients to create first-class dishes such as pork belly bao, smoked brisket, and the Umami Smash. The laid-back, underground restaurant hosts Happy Hour every weekday from 4 to 6 p.m., featuring food and drink specials. Join friends after work for sliders and a discounted draft beer. Return to the Public on Sundays for a Brunch Mary and charcuterie board.

Explore beyond the restaurant's doors into The Brickyard, voted Best Live Music Venue by the *Wichita Eagle* Reader's Choice Awards. Old Town's outdoor music venue hosts bands Thursday through Saturday. The lineup often includes crowd-pleasers like local favorites Lucky People, Rudy Love Jr., or Harrison Steele.

129 N Rock Island St., 316-263-4044
publicbrickyard.com

TIP
The eclectic restaurant decor includes repurposed items. See the indoor porch swing? Framed newspaper articles and album artwork cover the walls. The bathroom tiles are from the bank John Dillinger robbed.

ENJOY AWARD-WINNING MEDITERRANEAN FOOD
AT BELLA LUNA CAFÉ

While there are many restaurants that serve Mediterranean cuisine in town, only one has received top recognition in many categories from year to year. Bella Luna Café serves award-winning, fast-casual dining, and has earned the respect of locals for exceptional cuisine, especially the hummus.

In fact, people have declared their love for chef Matteo Taha's menu in writing. The wall above the kitchen in both locations is covered with testimonials from satisfied customers. The chef's menu is inspired by his Lebanese roots, featuring dishes like seafood pasta, curry entrees, kabobs, and gyros. The Fattoush salad pairs well with any entree choice. If you're in the mood to share a meal, order the Meza Sampler, a platter of five traditional Mediterranean appetizers.

2132 N Rock Rd., #107, 316-634-0008
2441 N Maize Rd., 316-613-3320
bellalunacafe.com

BE FIRST IN LINE FOR RIBS
AT PIG IN! PIG OUT!

Fans of Pig In! Pig Out! know that if they want to get their mitts on the barbecue joint's coveted ribs, they'd better arrive as soon as the place opens. Slabs of ribs are cut up for meat dinners and served alongside all the fixings on paper-lined metal trays. The competition-worthy BBQ meats have not only received high praise from locals, but also have earned Pig In! Pig Out! numerous ribbons and trophies. The rest of the menu checks all the boxes. Delicious side dishes? They've got them. Comforting cobblers? You bet. Banana pudding? Of course.

It's BBQ so good, people crave it year-round. Home chefs leave the cooking to the restaurant's catering service, PIPO BBQ, during the holidays. Meat lovers are known to arrive the day before Thanksgiving or Christmas to pick up smoked turkeys and hams.

1003 E 13th St. N, 316-263-7474
pipobbq.com

CHOOSE DINNER WITH A VIEW
AT NEWPORT GRILL

Newport Grill combines a sophisticated atmosphere with a picturesque view, unlike anything you'll find in the city. What could be better than savoring a plate of Hawaiian ahi tuna on the patio overlooking a waterfall?

The fine-dining establishment specializes in seafood shipped six days a week. The dinner menu gives patrons the option of pairing fresh-catch fish with two side dishes. Executive Chef Kevin Derks and his team turn out delectable dishes, from diver sea scallops to bistro steak.

Enjoy dining alfresco? The patio is the preferred place to enjoy a meal and drinks with friends. Jazz musicians keep the beat Thursday through Saturday. Stop by on Sunday for brunch or for Happy Hour, 3 p.m. to 6 p.m. and one hour before closing. Appetizers worth trying include East Coast Oysters and Rock Shrimp Cigars.

1900 N Rock Rd., 316-636-9555
newportgrill.com

LOVE YOUR LUNCH
AT THE MUSE CAFÉ

Have you ever wanted to find a quiet, scenic space to enjoy lunch away from the hustle and bustle of work-life? The Muse Café inside the Wichita Art Museum is the place. The moment you sit down at a sunlit table with a menu in hand, you immediately feel a sense of calm. The second-floor window view frames the museum's beautiful Art Garden below.

The lunch menu reflects a sense of health and well-being. Spinach and Beet Salad. Pan-Seared Salmon. Quiche of the Day. All of the menu selections are made with fresh ingredients and arrive at the table plated like a work of art. Chilled beverages range from bottled water to classic cocktails. Visiting the museum on the weekend? The cafe serves three signature brunch plates. The Egg-White Omelet is a crowd-pleaser.

1400 W Museum Blvd., 316-268-4973
wichitaartmuseum.org/cafe

GIVE IN
TO YOUR SWEET TOOTH
AT COCOA DOLCE

Can you imagine what it would be like to play with chocolate all day? The employees at Cocoa Dolce's downtown location get to conjure up their inner Willy Wonka seven days a week. You can live the sweet life, too. Watch certified chocolatiers make artisan chocolates, confections, and made-from-scratch pastries through the glass window that separates the production kitchen from the Sweet Lounge.

The shop is the perfect place to enjoy a specialty coffee on a date or when meeting a friend. Try the popular Java Shake. All three locations serve gelato, cheesecakes, and macarons. Visit during Happy Hour, Monday through Thursday, from 4 to 7 p.m., and get $1 off a beverage, including cocktails.

235 N St. Francis St., 316-854-3121
2132 N Rock Rd., Ste. 100, 316-866-2906
2441 N Maize Rd., Ste. 123, 316-866-6337
cocoadolce.com

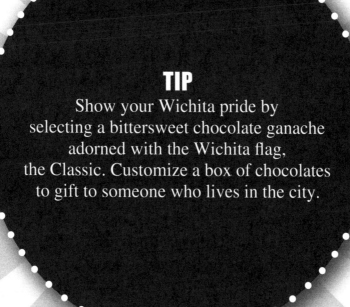

TIP

Show your Wichita pride by
selecting a bittersweet chocolate ganache
adorned with the Wichita flag,
the Classic. Customize a box of chocolates
to gift to someone who lives in the city.

ORDER FLAVORFUL PHO
AT LITTLE SAIGON

Wichita has voted Little Saigon's pho the best in the city numerous times, for a reason. Offering a taste of Vietnam, the restaurant has mastered the beef broth soup made with noodles and a choice of meat. It remains one of their signature dishes on a menu of favorites.

Aside from flavorful pho, you must experience other menu classics. The B4 Vermicelli Bowl is the second-most-ordered menu item. Grilled pork and an egg roll top a full bowl of noodles, bean sprouts, cilantro, and veggies. Pour fish sauce on it and you're on your way to Flavor Town. Diners in search of traditional Chinese dishes will also feel at home. The restaurant's food is consistently delicious.

Little Saigon's large dining room fills up for lunch and dinner, but the service is swift. Expect to enjoy a clean, relaxed atmosphere while you slurp noodles to your heart's content.

1015 N Broadway St., 316-265-0054
little-saigon-restaurant.cafes-city.com

SAY "BON APPETIT!"
AT GEORGES FRENCH BISTRO

For anyone who has ever yearned for an evening in France eating gourmet food and drinking wine, Georges French Bistro is the answer. The fine-dining restaurant's interior and sophisticated menu transports patrons to European elegance. You can choose between patio dining or white-linen service indoors—both deliver a memorable experience.

The cuisine represents the culture well, with classic bistro favorites like French onion soup, steak frites, escargot, and creme brûlée. Ask about the chef's special and the monthly sommelier selection. Specialty cocktails are handcrafted with care as diners enjoy gorgeous ambiance in a low-lit setting. Georges French Bistro receives top accolades. If you're celebrating a special occasion, the bistro is a go-to in the city for an intimate dinner or group gathering. The restaurant also serves breakfast and lunch.

4618 E Central Ave., Ste. 50, 316-831-1325
georgesfrenchbistro.com

SIP IN SECRET
AT DOCKUM

During the Prohibition era, when bars and saloons were shut down by law enforcement, speakeasies gave people a place to drink illegally. Dockum, a hidden speakeasy on the lower level of the historic Ambassador Hotel, transports visitors to an earlier time. Follow the signs. Patrons enter the nondescript door and walk down the marble staircase into a dimly lit room where handcrafted cocktails are served to the backdrop of jazz favorites.

Their only rule? "Be good to us and we'll spoil you." Part of the building was once a drug store, so it makes sense that the bartender, a.k.a. the dispensary's "pharmacist," mixes libations to cure all your ills. Hungry? You can order a meal from the upstairs restaurant, Siena Tuscan Steakhouse, and have it delivered to your table.

104 S Broadway St., 316-719-7119
dockum.com

TIP
Reservations are encouraged using the online booking system on Dockum's website, however, bar seating is first come, first served.

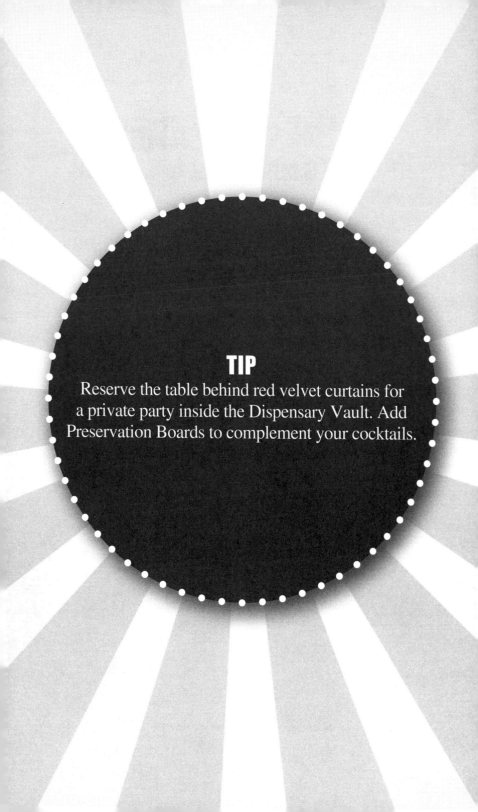

TIP

Reserve the table behind red velvet curtains for a private party inside the Dispensary Vault. Add Preservation Boards to complement your cocktails.

MAKE MEMORIES
AT MORT'S MARTINI & CIGAR BAR

Magnificent martinis. Perfected patio vibes. Mort's Martini & Cigar Bar serves an impressive list of over 160 creative cocktails in a relaxed atmosphere. A favorite Old Town hangout, located in a restored gas station, it has welcomed patrons for over two decades. Live music seekers love the patio. They jam to jazz or acoustic rock, or listen to singing songstresses, nearly every night of the week on the patio, while the martinis flow.

Visiting during the winter months? Ask your server to fire up the tabletop fire feature while you sip on a Presidential Martini or Dirty McNasty. Daily drink specials keep it interesting, especially on Martini Mondays when the classic cocktail is half-priced. The bar also touts a massive humidor. Cigar aficionados are welcomed to purchase one from the bar's selection and light it up at their table. For drinkers who work up an appetite, Mort's serves a shortlist of appetizers, and the popcorn machine is always on.

923 E 1st St. N, 316-262-1785
mortswichita.com

EAT A BURRITO
AT EL MEXICO CAFE

Locally owned and operated for over four decades, El Mexico Cafe is well-liked by locals for its smothered burritos, enchiladas, tacos, and grilled fajitas. The south Wichita restaurant attracts diners who expect consistently delicious food and friendly service. In fact, some residents have been eating there since they were kids.

Go hungry. You can expect large portions, with most entrees served on steaming-hot platters. The menu consists of Mexican cuisine standards, but everyone knows the shining star is the Deluxe Burrito. Two oversized tortillas are stuffed with slow-cooked beans and chile verde pork, topped with chili con carne and cheese. House-made flour tacos with savory beef and traditional toppings are a must-have. Consider planning your visit around their daily specials, and don't forget to order a margarita. On the rocks? With salt?

2544 S Seneca St., 316-558-8220
elmexicocafe.com

DEVOUR A MEAL
AT DOO-DAH DINER

"Walking in . . . !" The kitchen cook can be heard yelling orders at Doo-Dah Diner to the staff with the day's specials and breakfast entrees. Eager eaters sit in sparkly, vinyl-covered booths, awaiting plates with heaping portions. Daily specials often include dishes like Crab Cakes Benedict, pork belly and grits, and chicken or beef pot pie.

Doo-Dah Diner, named after the city's nickname, appeals to everyone. The restaurant is often filled with regulars hungry for comfort food, served with a smile six days a week. They've come to the right place for award-winning gourmet food. It is not a greasy spoon diner. The cooks arrive at 3 a.m. to prep the day's menu from scratch, using high-quality ingredients. They serve all-day breakfast, including popular entrees like Banana Bread French Toast and Crispy Corned Beef Hash.

206 E Kellogg St., 316-265-7011
doodahdiner.com

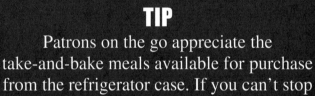

TIP

Patrons on the go appreciate the
take-and-bake meals available for purchase
from the refrigerator case. If you can't stop
inside for a bite to eat, drive up
to the pickup window or order carryout.

SAVOR THE FLAVOR
AT FREDDY'S FROZEN CUSTARD & STEAKBURGERS

"Grillin', Scoopin', Rockin'" is what the employees at Freddy's Frozen Custard & Steakburgers do best. The secret to the Wichita-based franchise's success is that they make delicious, old-fashioned steakburgers and smash them to perfection. Aside from the freshly cooked flavor, the burger's "skirt" is everything. Order the late founder's go-to meal, Freddy's Original Patty Melt and crispy shoestring fries, paired with Freddy's Famous Fry Sauce.

Warning: Leave room for dessert. The frozen custard is a fan favorite. A classic American treat, its flavor transports you back in time. Indulge in a Signature Turtle Sundae made with vanilla custard, hot fudge, hot caramel, toasted pecans, whipped cream, and a cherry.

The employees have fun at work, and it's contagious. You'll leave Freddy's with a full belly and wearing a smile.

TIP
If you crave Freddy's Famous Fry Sauce®, you can buy it on the restaurant's website. Don't forget a shaker of Freddy's Steakburger & Fry Seasoning™.

---

310 N Rock Rd., 316-691-9998

3450 S Meridian Ave., 316-223-4322

420 S Ridge Rd., Ste. 100, 316-260-2611

8621 W 21st St. N, 316-722-2299

11525 E 13th St. N, 316-440-5678

1845 Fairmount St., #56, 316-978-3477

300 S Sycamore St.

freddysusa.com

ENJOY
FOODIE FELLOWSHIP
AT FOOD TRUCKS AT THE FOUNTAINS

There is no better sight than two dozen food trucks serving hungry customers. Food Trucks at the Fountains in downtown Wichita is the place to be for foodies on the last Sunday of the month, May to October. While the lineup of food trucks varies from year to year, the midday event draws a crowd looking for concessions' favorites and ethnic street food.

Fans flock to Funky Monkey Munchies for Chino-Latin cuisine. The Flying Stove is famous for the Bronx Burger. The Rolling Greek serves a popular meat gyro. Have a sugar craving? The Food Trucks at the Fountains experience isn't complete without a gourmet cupcake from Brown Box Bakery.

520 S Main St., 316-219-6060
wichitawaterwalk.com/the-fountains-at-waterwalk

TIP

Look for the Liquid Fireworks®
the Fountains at WaterWalk to come alive,
providing for a picturesque landscape on the
hour. Five, 15-minute water shows take place
Thursday-Sunday at noon and
at 7, 8, 9, and 10 p.m.

ASK FOR EXTRA NAPKINS
AT DEMPSEY'S BURGER PUB

Holy moly, Dempsey's Burger Pub's burgers are good. Eat one combined with homemade truffle fries, and you may think you went to heaven after the first bite. They use non-traditional ingredients like bacon jam, Brie cheese, chorizo, or Korean slaw to ensure that each wagyu burger delivers a flavor explosion. Stacked with ingredients, they may require a fork and knife to consume. Pair the truffle fries with a dipping sauce like garlic aioli and they are out-of-this-world delicious.

Some of their one-off burger creations are so popular, they bring them back by popular demand for a limited time. Ask about the burger, According to Randy. If you need something to wash it down, order a Pineapple Jalapeño Margarita or locally made craft beer.

3700 E Douglas Ave., Ste. 78, 316-425-3831
dempseysburgerpub.com

TIP
Enjoy a sunny day on the patio or ask for seating downstairs to hang out in the restaurant's cozy basement.

SEND CHEERS TO WICHITA
AT JENNY DAWN CELLARS

When Jenny McDonald opened the doors to her urban winery, Jenny Dawn Cellars, Wichitans flocked to it. Located in historic Union Station, it offers award-winning varieties for wine lovers to enjoy in the tasting room or on a spacious patio. Her motto? "Let your moment begin!"

McDonald, a certified sommelier and winemaker, cut her chops in Napa Valley. Now, she serves vino enthusiasts handcrafted wines in a beautiful setting. Raise a glass of Union Station, a light-bodied chardonnay, with friends. Rather drink red? Enjoy Wichita Passion, a sweet red wine. If you can't decide on a wine, opt for a flight of two-ounce pours, complemented with a charcuterie or dessert plate from the small bites menu.

703 E Douglas Ave., Ste. 180, 316-633-3022
jennydawncellars.com

TIP
Serious sippers are invited to become members. They can store their favorite bottles at the perfect temperature in wine lockers to have at the ready when visiting the tasting room.

TOAST TO NEW FRIENDS
AT CENTRAL STANDARD BREWING

You may stop into Central Standard Brewing for a craft beer, but it's not uncommon to walk away having made new friends. The yard games beckon beer drinkers to play. Dog parents swap stories. Local musicians mingle with new fans.

A hipster hangout, the brewery earns style points for its choice of retro furniture and throwback board games. Patrons toast to good times with flavor-forward beers like Drop Top Caddy, Bling Blau, and Wizard of Hops. You're always guaranteed to see new beers listed on the letter board menu. Don't drink beer? Request a sangria or Mexican Coke.

The brewery knows how to party. Its anniversary block party, held in August, spills over into nearby Hyde Park and features live music, food trucks, and games for the kids. Show up on Sundays to enjoy patio vibes and jam to reggae music.

156 S Greenwood St., 316-260-8515
centralstandardbrewing.com

OTHER BREWERIES WITH OUTDOOR SEATING

**Hopping Gnome
Brewing Company**
quaint streetside patio
1710 E Douglas Ave.
316-771-2110
hoppinggnome.com

Limestone Beer Co.
inside Sweet Allie B's
restaurant with patio access
707 N Waco Ave., Ste. 105
316-729-6200
facebook.com/limestonebeerco

**Nortons
Brewing Company**
expansive, dog-friendly
outdoor seating
125 St. Francis St.
316-425-9009
nortonsbrewing.com

Third Place Brewing
informal outdoor seating
630 E Douglas Ave.
316-833-2873
thirdplacebrew.com

**PourHouse by
Walnut River Brewing Co.**
spacious patio facing
historic Union Station
711 E Douglas Ave., Ste. 105
316-260-4897
pourhouseict.com

**Wichita Brewing Co.
& Pizzeria**
patio seating at both locations
8815 W 13th St., Ste. 100
316-440-2885
535 N Woodlawn St.
316-440-4885
wichitabrew.com

River City Brewing Co.
second-story balcony
seating above
Old Town's square
150 N Mosley St.
316-263-2739
rivercitybrewingco.com

GO BIG WITH A BLOODY MARY
AT BITE ME BBQ

Revered for its ginormous Bloody Mary, Bite Me BBQ attracts meat lovers looking to take their dining experience to new heights. The towering cocktail arrives at the table in a beer mug with skewers of smoked barbecue and veggies. One look at it and your mouth begins to water. You won't find a bigger, bolder Bloody Mary in town. Loaded with a sparerib, hot link, burnt end, cheese cubes, celery, olives, cherry tomatoes, and cucumbers, it's a meal on its own.

The cocktail is the gateway to a delicious BBQ journey. If you're still hungry, dive into a slab of ribs—voted one of the best in the state by *Kansas! Magazine*. The slow-smoked brisket and pulled pork are equally as tasty. The laid-back establishment also serves prime rib dinners on Friday and Saturday nights until the prime rib runs out.

132 N St. Francis St., 316-729-2904
biteme-bbq.com

SIP SUDS ON A SWING
AT NORTONS BREWING COMPANY

Beer devotees appreciate Nortons Brewing Company's ever-changing taps and atmosphere. The only thing they love more? The beer garden. Sip suds on a porch swing while listening to bands like the Beastie Boys playing over the speakers. Craft beers like Polkadot Princess or Deez Hops make a game of cornhole a lot more fun.

Families find the patio an inviting space as well. Dog parents are encouraged to bring their four-legged friends to play among giddy kids on the lawn. With all the activity, it's easy to work up an appetite. The menu is adventurous. Diners appreciate noshing on Bacon Crack, Parmesan Garlic Fries, and Fried Pickles, for starters. Main menu stars like the Grizzled Cheese sandwich or the Norton Burger are solid choices. Fight for your right to devour a funnel cake before heading home.

125 N St. Francis St., 316-425-9009
nortonsbrewing.com

TIP
Check out the massive mural near the beer garden's entrance facing St. Francis Street. It's the ideal backdrop for a group photo.

SIT AT
THE SODA FOUNTAIN
AT OLD MILL TASTY SHOP

There is probably no better restaurant in Wichita to experience the city's history firsthand than Old Mill Tasty Shop. Diners have enjoyed sitting at the marble counter for fountain service and tasty sandwiches since 1932. The retro interior and old-fashioned ice cream specialties make a visit to the restaurant like a step back in time. The Wright family's recipe for success is serving excellent food with a side of hospitality. The staff, including longtime waitress Gale Cowan, is known for its enthusiastic nature.

Couples cuddle up in booths, kids hover over sundaes, and parents dive into menu favorites. Daily Blue Plate specials like chicken-fried chicken, lasagna, enchiladas, and meatloaf keep regulars coming back for big portions. You're likely to find Cajun cuisine on Fat Tuesday or chocolate cake on Valentine's Day.

604 E Douglas Ave., 316-264-6500
oldmilltastyshop.com

TIP

Order the chili. The Wright's recipe
has taken the Wagonmasters Downtown
Chili Cookoff Grand Champion prize.
It pairs nicely with a milkshake.

START YOUR DAY
AT REVERIE ROASTERS

You've heard the expression, "But first, coffee." Stopping into Reverie Roasters's flagship location for a delicious coffee is a draw for city dwellers who prefer to kickstart their day with a caffeine buzz. Coffee is a number-one priority for one of the city's leading bean roasters.

Maybe it's the modern industrial ambiance. Perhaps it's the fresh-baked pastries or biscuits and gravy. Whatever it is, it works. After ordering an espresso or Pistachio Rose Latté, grab a seat underneath the gold-painted mural. The cultural hub is an ideal place to nestle into a table for conversation with a friend or colleague. Visiting alone? Bring your knitting needles, a book, or a laptop. It's not uncommon to see patrons polishing their hobbies or at work with a hot tea or coffee within reach.

2202 E Douglas Ave., 316-201-1144
reverieroasters.com

TIP

Reverie Roasters' purists can sign up for a subscription to have coffee shipped to their door weekly, bi-weekly, or monthly. Choose from six coffee varieties, whole bean or ground, and 12 ounces or five pounds. They also offer catered coffee services if you're hosting a party.

BELLY UP TO THE BAR
AT THE ANCHOR

A popular neighborhood bar and grill, The Anchor serves a long list of craft beers, cocktails, and gastropub menu favorites. It was voted Kansas's Best Beer Bar 2019 by CraftBeer.com readers. With over 20 taps and a refrigerator full of craft beer sourced from Kansas to Canada, hopheads feel at home. Sit at the copper-top bar with a beer or cocktail in hand and watch as the fast-moving kitchen staff prepares piled-high portions.

The bar and grill takes food seriously. Sandwich lovers dig the Original Beef Reuben on rye. Unafraid of spicy heat? Order the Burn Notice Wings! to kick it up a notch. The BBQ Mac Attack and Dos Tacos make dinner a delight.

1109 E Douglas Ave., 316-260-8989
anchorwichita.com

TIP
The Anchor Meat Market next door sells Kansas heritage, premium meats. The specialty butcher shop also sells take-and-make pasta kits on Wednesdays. Stock up on artisan cheese, homemade soup, bottled wine, and local produce.

BETTER YOUR BRUNCH
AT THE BELMONT

The place to enjoy a superior brunch in Wichita is The Belmont. Executive Chef Jacob Cook uses fresh ingredients sourced from Kansas farms. Devour main dishes such as crispy almond waffles, stacked croissant sandwiches, and sourdough toast piled high with avocado and tabbouleh. Brunch boozers appreciate five signature cocktails, ranging from whiskey-based coffee drinks to fizzy prosecco drinks.

Weather permitting, the staff raises the garage doors to bring the outside indoors. While patio seating is first-come, first-serve, it is one of the better seats in the house for its view of the College Hill neighborhood. The Belmont's interior has mid-century modern vibes. If you're waiting for a table, walk a few doors down to The Flower Shop, an additional space operated by the restaurant that serves drinks.

3555 E Douglas Ave., 316-477-3555
thebelmontks.com

TIP
Brunch service begins at 10 a.m. If it's after 6 p.m. on Sunday, it's still Happy Hour. Ask about drink specials including cocktails, select beers, and wine all day long.

MUSIC
AND ENTERTAINMENT

TRACK DOWN MURALS
IN THE DOUGLAS DESIGN DISTRICT

The Douglas Design District is the home of over 100 vibrant murals. Since 2015, Avenue Art Days has given local artists a canvas to express their creativity. The subject matter of each one varies. Some of the murals highlight what the city is known for, from aviation manufacturing to the Wichita flag. If you're scouting for a family photo location, the oversized masterpieces are the ideal backdrop.

The artwork extends beyond murals. Look closely around corners and down alleyways. The public art installations also include painted trash cans, park benches, and doors. To take a self-guided tour of all of the murals, use the free Avenue Art Days Mural Map app to navigate your route. Check the website for information about upcoming Avenue Art Days events that allow visitors to meet artists and see newly unveiled installations.

E Douglas St., between Washington Blvd. and Oliver St.
avenueartdays.com

GO TRICK-OR-TREATING
IN COLLEGE HILL

Wichita's east side neighborhood, College Hill, transforms during the holidays. The community celebrates Halloween unlike any other in the city. As soon as the air goes crisp, homeowners begin decorating. Front yards, second-floor windows, and driveways are adorned with ghoulish displays.

A popular place for trick-or-treating, the community sets the scene for a frighteningly good time. Drivers stop their cars to admire lawn decor. Parents encourage kids to ring doorbells. One of the city's top Halloween attractions, College Hill's homeowners take pride in their elaborate decorations. Have you seen the yard filled with dolls? What about the lawn covered in illuminated jack-o'-lanterns? Forget the candy. The Halloween decorations are the treat.

College Hill Neighborhood
collegehillneighborhood.com

WATCH A MOVIE
AT NAFTZGER PARK

Bring your blankets and lawn chairs to Naftzger Park—it's family movie night! The newly renovated park, nestled between downtown and Old Town, is a hip gathering space for the community. Nothing brings people together like a movie on a large digital screen under the stars.

Don't worry about buying a ticket, because admission is free. Save your money for visiting a food truck or nearby Peace Love & Pie, which serves delectable desserts. Kids love playing yard games and running around on the Astroturf field. All family members are welcome—even leashed dogs! Naftzger Park has a small, designated play area where Fido and his friends can hang on the hill.

Check the Facebook page for upcoming events, which often include concerts, dance performances, exercise classes, and shop-local markets.

601 E Douglas Ave., 316-268-4124
wichita.gov/parkandrec/naftzgerpark

LISTEN
TO THE WICHITA
SYMPHONY ORCHESTRA

The crescendo. The melody. The beautiful sounds of the Wichita Symphony Orchestra are unmistakable. Since 1944, some of the city's most talented musicians have delighted audiences at Century II Performing Arts & Convention Center. Experience a night on the town unlike any other. There is no dress code, so come as you are to listen to pops, masterworks, or community performances. Can't decide what concert to attend for the first time? Use the website's "choose a playlist" option that matches your personality with upcoming concert suggestions tailored to you.

The symphony also brings the music to the community. You'll often find musicians playing for appreciative crowds in parks and at special events, making music accessible to everyone. It's not uncommon to hear the sounds of the symphony at places like Botanica, Old Cowtown, and Naftzger Park.

225 W Douglas Ave., 316-267-7658
wichitasymphony.org

GAZE AT THE GARDENS
AT BOTANICA

Escaping to Botanica gives visitors a chance to appreciate nature's beauty in the heart of the city. Fun awaits families at the Downing Children's Garden, Butterfly House, and Chinese Garden of Friendship. Sidewalks wind sightseers through thematic gardens filled with seasonal botanicals. Bronze sculptures peek out above rows of roses and blankets of black-eyed Susans.

The horticultural center is revered for its warm-weather events. Small groups gather for Yoga in the Gardens. Friends mingle at Blooms, Brews, and Bloody Marys. Concerts entertain families on the Grand Lawn. The Alexander Bee House hosts a honey tasting experience in late summer. When temperatures begin to drop, tickets for Illuminations, a holiday light display tour, sell quickly.

701 Amidon St., 316-264-0448
botanica.org

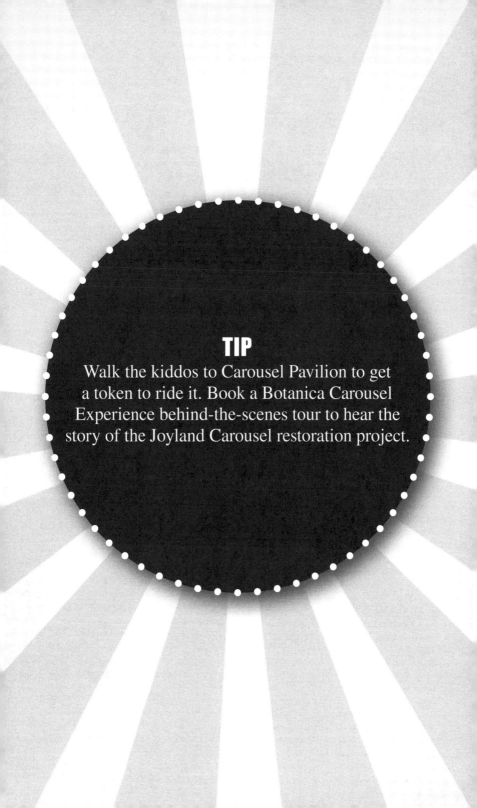

TIP

Walk the kiddos to Carousel Pavilion to get a token to ride it. Book a Botanica Carousel Experience behind-the-scenes tour to hear the story of the Joyland Carousel restoration project.

GET FIRED UP
AT WAGONMASTERS
DOWNTOWN CHILI COOKOFF

Chiliheads show up to Douglas Avenue and St. Francis Street in hopes of feeling the burn at the Wagonmasters Downtown Chili Cookoff every September. Over 80 teams duke it out for the title of the best chili in the Midwest. At noon, the firing of the cannon signals the official start of the festival.

Heat seekers purchase $5 tasting kits. The proceeds go to fund Good Life Grants that pay it forward to local charities and nonprofit organizations. Each kit includes a spoon, Wet-Nap, bracelet, and a bean used for casting a vote for the People's Choice Award. There are seven categories to compete in, ranging from No Beans About It to Chili For Charity.

Chili mania continues as teams compete for Best Booth by decorating their tailgate tents and dressing in costume. The Pepper Eating Contest puts contestants in the hot seat to find out who can eat as many jalapeños as possible in five minutes. The winner gets $100.

Douglas Ave. and St. Francis St.
wagonmasters.org/chili-cookoff

FIND
THE KEEPERS ON PARADE

The Keepers on Parade, micro versions of the iconic *Keeper of the Plains* statue located downtown, are placed all over the city. Together Wichita's public art project commissions the work of local painters to adorn 10-foot-tall fiberglass replicas with an approved design.

Each mini statue is unique, and many of the artists connect their individual designs to the location where their statue stands. Some Keepers on Parade are at home indoors in places like Northeast Magnet High School, while others are placed outdoors at entrances like the one at the Sedgwick County Zoo.

Finding the statues is a free, family-friendly activity that can be done year-round. New statues are being added to the collection. Choose a good weather day and set out to find them all using the Keeper 150 Sculpture Project's interactive map. Use #Keeper150 in your social media posts.

316-268-6268
togetherwichita.com/keepers-on-parade

TAKE IN THE ACOUSTICS
AT THE COTILLION

If you want to hear your favorite band play live, The Cotillion's acoustics deliver sound unlike any venue in town. Since opening night on December 7, 1960, the "Round Mound of Sound" has hosted concerts, dances, and special events for up to 2,000 people at a time. The building's circular design and 24-foot-high dome ceiling optimizes acoustics for audiences.

Everyone who is anyone has played at The Cotillion. The venue has hosted sold-out shows for all types of musicians, from Louis Armstrong to Willie Nelson. Acts like Etta James, Modest Mouse, and Stone Temple Pilots have kept concertgoers on their feet. Who would you love to hear play there? The Cotillion is probably hosting them soon.

11120 W Kellogg St., 316-722-4021
thecotillion.com

TIP

Doors typically open one hour prior to the event time, so arrive early to score the best parking spot and seats indoors.

All tickets are general admission.

Scope out the place in advance using 360-degree virtual tour links on the website.

WATCH A SUNRISE
AT THE LARGEST MURAL IN THE WORLD

It's unlike anything you've seen before, and it's worthy of a visit. The Beachner Grain Elevator mural, painted by Latin American urban artist GLeo, is the largest mural in the world painted by a single artist. To see its vibrant colors aglow at sunrise is a sight to behold.

The east-facing mural, a.k.a. *The Original Dream*, is part of a larger initiative to connect two neighborhoods, the Horizontes Project. Who are the individuals portrayed in GLeo's street art? They represent the people of the community, past and present. According to GLeo, they honor "the beauty of migrating as a fundamental right." To navigate to the mural, park your car near 21st and Broadway streets and walk to it. Located in an industrial area of North Wichita, the neighborhood also is home to over 20 other murals by various artists.

519 E 20th St. N
horizontes-project.com/port/gleo

CATCH A MOVIE
AT STARLITE DRIVE-IN

Do you remember watching a movie with your family at the drive-in, only to rush to the snack bar at intermission? Relive the nostalgic experience at Starlite Drive-In.

You can expect double and triple features on weekends. Stay tuned for special events like Scary Movie Monday and Encore Drive-In Nights featuring music acts. Can't get enough? The drive-in is open seven days a week during the summer. Whether you buy individual tickets or carload tickets, tickets must be purchased at the box office the night of the showing. Moviegoers can arrive one hour before the show begins. After parking, flick fanatics listen to the movie via FM radio or mobile phone app. Don't bother packing snacks. Walk to the concession stand to purchase tasty treats like homemade cotton candy, fresh popcorn, and funnel cakes.

3900 S Hydraulic St., 316-524-2424
starlitefun.com

ROAR WITH LAUGHTER
AT THE LOONY BIN COMEDY CLUB

They say laughter is the best medicine. The Loony Bin Comedy Club dishes out doses of high-energy hilarity to crowds most Wednesdays and every Thursday, Friday, and Saturday. Touring comedians keep audiences in stitches. Whether you're a fan of improv, open mic nights, or polished comics, the Loony Bin Comedy Club delivers. Audiences can expect two to three comics on weekends.

The club's atmosphere is electric. Waitresses keep spirits high by delivering signature cocktails like The Lobotomy, a rite of passage for patrons. As the dinner hour approaches, patrons can enjoy appetizers like Loaded Nachos and Homemade Spud Skins. The menu is nothing to laugh at, either. Baked Bird Bowls, shrimp scampi, and chicken salad keep audience members happy.

215 N St. Francis St., 316-618-4242
wichita.loonybincomedy.com

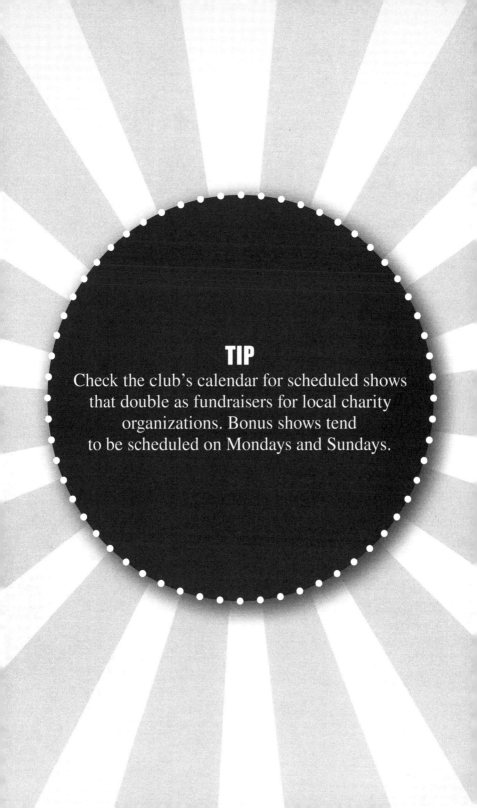

TIP

Check the club's calendar for scheduled shows that double as fundraisers for local charity organizations. Bonus shows tend to be scheduled on Mondays and Sundays.

EXPLORE YOUR CREATIVE SIDE
AT CITYARTS

It's likely that you'll feel inspired and want to create art after perusing CityArts's galleries. Fortunately, the center offers adult workshops in a variety of subjects like pottery, photography, glassblowing, drawing, painting, mixed media, and silversmithing. Young creatives can choose from classes especially from them. Some classes are one-day sessions, while others last multiple weeks.

If you'd like others to join in on the artistic experience with you, CityArts offers a team-building opportunity for coworkers and groups of all kinds. Hands-on activities like glassblowing reinforce problem-solving skills and creative thinking among colleagues. While art lessons include a fee, CityArts's galleries are open to the public to view at no cost. Stay tuned for the student-instructor show, when workshop creations are on display in the main gallery.

334 N Mead St., 316-350-3245
wichita.gov/cityarts

CELEBRATE ST. PATRICK'S DAY
AT THE ARTICHOKE SANDWICHBAR

Let the countdown to a Wichita tradition begin! The Artichoke Sandwichbar hosts a legendary party for St. Patrick's Day, where cold Guinness flows like a stream and Celtic musicians play authentic folk music. Never missing a beat, the Irish step dancers keep the patio party lively.

What's a celebration without food? The Irish dive bar's Reuben sandwich and tasty Mulligan stew are on the menu. Not a fan of corned beef? Order The Famous #8 Sandwich—it's considered "the most popular sandwich in Wichita." The "restaurant by day and full by night" finds festive ways to honor the holiday. A mini leprechaun, Patrick, is hidden around the bar. Find it and you win a prize. Touch the leprechaun prints on the Blarney Stone outside of the bar's entrance. Good luck will follow you all day.

811 N Broadway St., 316-263-9164
artichokesandwichbar.com

VIEW A LIVE SHOW
AT THE ORPHEUM

There is something special about seeing a concert, comedian, or theatrical performance at The Orpheum. If you've been there, you can attest to the uniqueness of the experience. Built in 1922, it remains one of 17 Orpheum theaters remaining in the country. Additionally, it was the first atmospheric theater in the US and remains the oldest one still standing. Once a vaudeville theater, today it hosts performances by well-known musical acts and performers.

From the moment you walk inside, the setting envelops you. Performances are made better because of the theatre's acoustics and unobstructed view. Attending a show? Look up after the lights go down. Architect John Eberson designed the 1200-plus-seat auditorium to resemble a Spanish courtyard, down to its night sky, plaster moldings, and wall sconces. On the National Register of Historic Places, it's worthy of a visit.

200 N Broadway St., 316-263-0884
wichitaorpheum.com

BECOME A FAN
OF MUSIC THEATRE OF WICHITA

Lively. Invigorating. High-energy. From the props and costumes to the full orchestra, Music Theatre of Wichita consistently delivers top-notch performances equal to or better than musicals you'd see in larger cities. Broadway actors often join productions as guest stars. As they say, "This is where you see the Broadway stars of today and tomorrow."

The audience watches talented performers sing and dance against elaborate backdrops bringing stories to life. *Fiddler on the Roof*, *Music Man*, *Oklahoma!*, and *The Sound of Music* are just a sampling of the shows that have been performed to appreciative audiences. The alumni concerts, as well as the holiday special show, are not to be missed.

While most of the shows take place at Century II Performing Arts & Convention Center, the actors also hit the stage at smaller venues like Capitol Federal Amphitheater in Andover and downtown's Naftzger Park.

225 W Douglas Ave., 316-265-3107
mtwichita.org

REVEL
IN THE WICHITA RIVERFEST

Since 1972, the annual Riverfest has been a treasure for those seeking summer fun. People come out in droves to enjoy outdoor events, devour food court delights, and rock out to headliner performances.

Downtown Wichita comes alive, and the list of family-friendly events is long. Bathtub races on the Arkansas River are a long-standing tradition. Onlookers watch the Sundown Parade with funnel cakes and Pronto Pups in hand. The Classic Car Show is a must-stop for motorheads. Racers compete at their best in The River Run. The annual event ends with the Capitol Federal Fireworks show reflecting on the Arkansas River.

Attendees need to purchase a button to take part in all of the activities and concerts. A comprehensive schedule of events is available on the festival's official mobile app.

Downtown Wichita, 316-267-2817
wichitariverfest.com

TIP

Consider yourself a sleuth? Participate in the Eagle Medallion Hunt®, a time-honored River Festival tradition. Use daily published clues in the *Wichita Eagle* to figure out where the medallion is hidden within Sedgwick County. The winner takes home $1,000.

DISCOVER A FAVORITE FLICK
AT TALLGRASS FILM FESTIVAL

Tallgrass Film Festival makes it possible for movie buffs to watch original stories play out on the screen in the form of short films, documentaries, and features. "Stubbornly Independent" since 2003, the five-day cinematic festival welcomes filmmakers, films, and fans to downtown Wichita every October. But it's more than your average movie festival. *MovieMaker Magazine* named Tallgrass Film Festival among "50 Festivals Worth the Entry Fee."

The nonprofit festival brings film fans together to celebrate smaller-budget moviemaking. Directors and actors often answer questions from the audience. It's a week of full-tilt fun. While you can purchase single tickets to movie showings, the TALLPass grants VIP access to the entire lineup of films, exclusive events, and the festival's parties. Check the website for Virtual Screening Room access, open to ticket holders.

316-303-9292
tallgrassfilm.org

SEE THE BRONZE SCULPTURES
ON DOUGLAS AVENUE

Barefoot Business Man. Little Girl with Horse and Pig. Boy on Scooter. What do these people have in common? They represent three of the 31 bronze sculptures by artist Georgia Gerber, positioned along Douglas Avenue. Part of an urban restoration movement, the commissioned public art project's goal was to attract passersby and start conversations.

Residents and visitors alike take photos with the sculptures. Which life-size sculpture will become your favorite? One, in particular, has drawn national attention for its historic reference to the 1958 Dockum Drugstore lunch counter sit-in. The bronze soda fountain sculpture depicts the Black student-led effort to end segregation, a victorious one, which prompted other retail stores to change their policies.

Douglas Ave. between Main St. and Topeka Ave., 316-264-6005
downtownwichita.org

PARTY DOWN
AT BRADLEY FAIR'S
SUMMER CONCERT SERIES

For five weeks during the summer, Bradley Fair shopping plaza hosts live music on Thursdays as the sun sets. The June-July concert series includes a lineup of musicians and local talent, ranging from jazz keyboardists to vocalists. The fun starts the moment the first music note is played and commences after the sun goes down. People dance near the stage. The outdoor scene becomes one of the liveliest venues of the summer. Be ready! Musicians are known to leave the stage and play among the crowd.

Who's invited? Everyone! Families, couples, and friends bring lawn chairs and blankets to enjoy lakeside picnic-style seating. Reserved plaza seating is available on a limited basis for concertgoers who register in advance. Either location is a delightful place to enjoy a meal alfresco to the energizing sound of high-caliber musicians.

2000 N Rock Rd., 316-630-9990
bradleyfair.com/event/the-summer-concert-series

SING IN UNISON
AT INTRUST BANK ARENA

Situated in the middle of downtown, INTRUST Bank Arena plays host to mega bands and well-known artists, from Guns N' Roses to Garth Brooks. When the moment arrives and spectators are singing in unison, illuminated by stage lights, it's a special place to be. Imagine over 6,000 fans matching pitch, word for word. Whether you're swaying to songs in the front row or seated near the rafters, the energy in the arena can be felt no matter where you sit.

One look at the arena's event calendar and you'll discover there is even more to love. When a music performance isn't on the bill, the arena hosts sports competitions like the NCAA Division I Basketball Championships, World Wrestling Entertainment Smackdown, and the Wichita Thunder. Dance troupes, comedians, and Sesame Street characters have all taken the stage at INTRUST Bank Arena.

500 E Waterman St., 316-440-9000
intrustbankarena.com

VIEW ONE-OF-A-KIND ARTWORK
AT FIRST FRIDAY GALLERY CRAWL

In an effort to support local artists, galleries open their doors and invite the public to visit during First Friday Gallery Crawl at no cost each month. Artists display their work or present at closing receptions in galleries downtown and throughout the city. What started as a grassroots movement has evolved into a strong following of art aficionados and first-time gallery patrons going from place to place to view art exhibits. From breweries to sophisticated art galleries and outdoor spaces to boutiques, each location is as unique as the art on showcase. Art seekers can expect to see one-of-a-kind pieces, observe artist demonstrations, and on occasion, listen to live music. Gallery hours vary.

316-264-6005
firstfridayict.org

TIP

First Friday opening art receptions are
sometimes hosted in unlikely locations, like KU
School of Medicine-Wichita. Add William J.
Reals Gallery of Art, 1010 North Kansas Street,
to your tour. The gallery is free to visit from
9 a.m.-4 p.m., Monday-Friday.

WATCH FIREWORKS
FROM THE BANK OF
THE ARKANSAS RIVER

Crackle! Bang! Shimmer! There's no better seat in the city to watch fireworks from than the bank of the Arkansas River. Red, White, & BOOM!, Wind Surge baseball games, and the Riverfest put on massive pyrotechnic shows, illuminating the downtown skyline. The reflection of the brightly lit colors on the water is a sight to behold.

Red, White & BOOM! celebrates the nation's independence at Riverfront Stadium on July 4 with free admission, live music, and games for the kids. Wind Surge postgame fireworks give baseball fans a show from the comfort of their seats, but the display can also be enjoyed from the river's vantage point. Wichita's favorite summer party, Riverfest, kicks off and concludes with bursts of color in the night sky. Grab a blanket or a lawn chair and pick your spot along the Arkansas River for an up-close view. It's spectacular.

Downtown Wichita
wichitaparksfoundation.org
milb.com/wichita/ballpark

PRESS PLAY
AT THE ARCADE

Have you mastered Pac-Man? Nearly perfected Galaga? The Arcade is an electronic playground for video game fans.

The dimly lit room is a sensory overload. Gamers get serious about Donkey Kong and Golden Tee. The fast-firing sounds of Asteroids and Centipede compete with radio hits playing from the overhead speaker. Colorful lights flash on the nearby pinball machines. It's a fun place to be as everyone battles for the highest score on over 77 games and 13 pinball machines.

Admission is $10 per person to play as long as you want, $8 for kids 10 and under. All arcade games are set to free play. Consider yourself a pinball wizard? It's only 50 cents per play. Single- and multi-player games are available. Inquire about private party reservations for up to 100 guests.

139 N Mead St., 316-844-0100
thearcadewichita.com

GET HANDS-ON
AT EXPLORATION PLACE

Exploration Place is where kids love to learn and adults love to feel like kids again. The science museum caters to those who want to dive deep into the reasons why and how things work. Permanent exhibits like Design Build Fly, Where Kids Rule, and Explore Kansas ignite your curiosity as you interact with hands-on activities.

Take exploration to another level. Buy a ticket to a show in the Dome Theater and Planetarium for an immersive 360-degree viewing of topics ranging from animal behavior to space exploration. The sound system will amaze you. Don't miss Orbit Academy, a 30-minute live science show about space travel.

300 N McLean Blvd., 316-660-0600
exploration.org

TIP

Visit Exploration Place on a summer evening for Food Truck Thursdays, when the parking lot fills with families enjoying a meal, live music, and games. The evening comes to a close when the Ring of Fire ignites in front of the *Keeper of the Plains*.

ROCK OUT UNDER THE STARS
AT WAVE

Imagine for a moment that you're relaxing in an outdoor lounge setting, surrounded by fellow music lovers. Enlarge it and add a killer sound system and a massive stage. Now, invite your favorite band to play there. You have all the makings of Wave, a concert venue and community space.

Although the venue also has an indoor performance space with a bar, people dig the outdoor scene, especially when rocking out under the night sky to bands with major star quality. Concert fans have jammed to all genres of music, from Snoop Dogg to the Dropkick Murphys.

Wave also serves up excellent food and drink. Adiós Nachoria prepares Mexican dishes with fresh ingredients, turning out enchiladas, tostadas, and of course, stacked nachos. The bar's craft beer game is legit and includes locally made brews.

650 E 2nd St., 316-260-5141
waveict.com

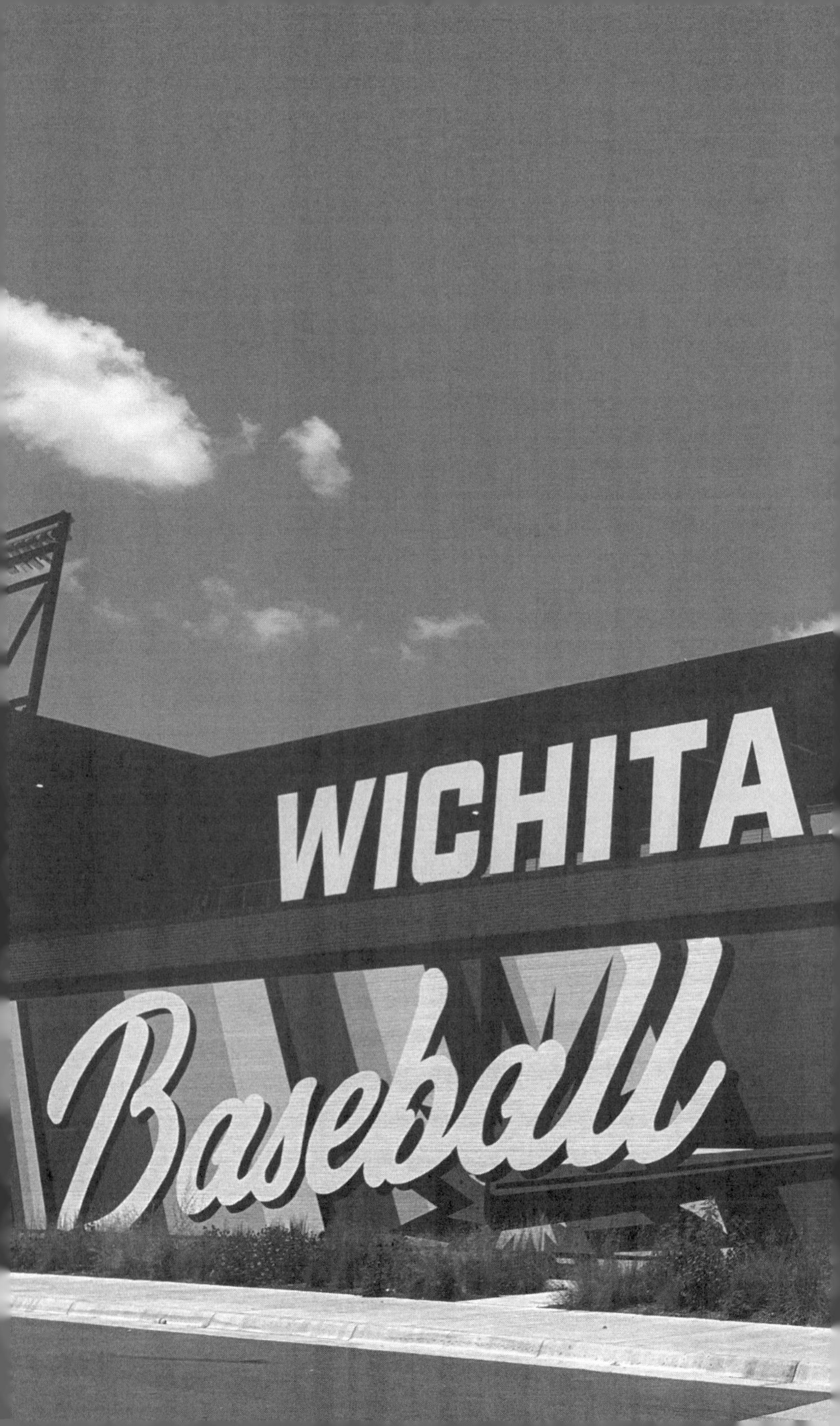
WICHITA
Baseball

SPORTS
AND RECREATION

CHEER ON
WICHITA STATE UNIVERSITY
MEN'S SHOCKER BASKETBALL

The atmosphere in Charles Koch Arena during a Wichita State University Men's Shocker Basketball game is electric. The place pulsates with energy (a.k.a. Shocker Madness) as fans cheer on the home team in The Roundhouse. When the boys in black and yellow hit the court, a packed arena erupts with excitement. Every dunk, every steal, they get LOUD.

You can expect high-energy entertainment until the clock runs down. The spirit squad gets fans on their feet and the student band brings the beats. Halftime delivers a fun time, giving spectators a chance to win prizes or catch flying T-shirts. Not to be missed, Senior Day is a celebration unlike any other, when players are recognized by family, friends, and fans. Whether it's a regular-season game or a championship battle, the community shows up for a thrilling display of athleticism.

1845 Fairmount St., 316-978-3267
goshockers.com/sports/mens-basketball

SPORTS BARS TO WATCH THE GAME

Deano's Grill & Tapworks
Restaurant and bar with walls of TVs
9747 E 21st St. N, Ste. 101, 316-977-7107
deanosict.com

Side Pockets Restaurant & Sports Bar
Pool hall with private event space
614 S Tyler Rd., 316-729-4000
sidepocketswichita.com

Emerson Biggin's Sports Bar and Grill
Big TVs and big food portions
808 E Douglas Ave., 316-303-9800
emersonbiggins.com

2330 N Maize Rd., Ste. 100, 316-866-2577
bigginswest.com

Walt's
Hometown atmosphere
7732 E Central Ave., 316-691-8800
waltseast.com

Pumphouse
Converted filling station
825 E 2nd St. N, 316-262-7867
pumphousewichita.com

Heroes Sports Bar & Grill
In historic Old Town
117 N Mosley St., 316-264-4376
facebook.com/heroessportsbar

LACE UP YOUR SKATES
AT WICHITA ICE CENTER

Have you ever watched a hockey player or figure skater on the ice and wondered how they make it look so easy? Since 1996, Wichita Ice Center has hosted beginner to advanced skaters who want to enjoy the winter pastime year-round. The ice sports destination features Olympic and NHL rinks, party rooms, a restaurant, and a pro shop. The best time to leisurely skate or practice your pirouettes is during Public Skate, which takes place midday, every day. Evening skate sessions are Tuesdays, Fridays, and Saturdays.

Don't worry if ice skating doesn't come naturally to you. The center provides lessons from experienced instructors. For skaters who want to tap into their competitive side, both youth and adult leagues are available.

505 W Maple St., 316-337-9199
wichitaicecenter.com

FIND YOUR FUN
AT O. J. WATSON PARK

O. J. Watson Park is where families love to explore. The 119-acre space includes a 40-acre lake that provides an endless good time for people of all ages. Kids will beg to play on one of three playgrounds. Don't be surprised if they want to ride the miniature train. It's open to all ages with the purchase of a ticket. Children smile ear-to-ear while riding live ponies, an opportunity for parents to snap photos.

In the mood for a laid-back park experience? Polish your putting skills on the 18-hole miniature golf course or enjoy the lake's scenery from a paddleboat or kayak. Back on land, anglers can drop a line into one of two fishing lakes on-site. When it's picnic time, cooking burgers on an available charcoal grill or visiting the concessions stand makes mealtime easy.

3022 S McLean Blvd., 316-529-9940
wichita.gov/parkandrec/watsonpark

GET ROWDY
AT A WICHITA THUNDER HOCKEY GAME

Screaming fans, the slap of the puck, and the roar of the buzzer set the scene at Wichita Thunder hockey games. The East Coast Hockey League (ECHL) minor league team battles AA-level teams on the ice in front of excited fans at INTRUST Bank Arena from October to April.

For three decades, a loyal following of fans has cheered for the home team. The fan experience is unmistakable. Spectators don team colors, applaud with inflatable noisemakers, a.k.a. "thunder sticks," and on occasion, rattle the rink's glass with fervor. The energy remains high as the Ice Girls keep fans entertained between halves, dancing in the center of the rink.

500 E Waterman St., 316-264-4625
wichitathunder.com

TIP

Promotional games add bonus entertainment to the schedule, with themed nights like Teddy Bear Toss and Military Appreciation Night. On #ILoveWichita Night, players show their city pride by wearing a Wichita flag-themed jersey. The first 500 fans in the door receive a complimentary gift.

BOWL A PERFECT GAME
AT SENECA BOWL

In a league of its own, Seneca Bowl has hosted amateur and professional players in search of perfecting their game for years on the city's south side. The well-maintained bowling alley has over 20 lanes open for play every day of the week at an affordable price. It's fun for the entire family. Bring the kids for bumper bowling or to enjoy the mini arcade. Celebrating a good game with friends? Toast with an adult beverage served from the bar. The kitchen is known for serving up delicious burgers.

The lanes are open for glow-in-the-dark Cosmic Bowling on Friday and Saturday nights—also a New Year's Eve tradition. Pin hitters appreciate All You Can Bowl sessions during the day: Monday through Friday, 11 a.m.-2 p.m.; Tuesday and Wednesday, 7-10 p.m.

1909 S Seneca St., 316-267-7301
senecabowl.net

TIP
Wichita State University's bowling teams have won numerous national titles—the most in collegiate bowling history. They offer camps for bowlers ages 10–18. wichita.edu/athletics/bowling

TAKE TO THE TRAILS
AT SEDGWICK COUNTY PARK

When you're in search of an outdoor setting to enjoy good weather while burning calories, the paved trails at Sedgwick County Park are an ideal place to walk, bike, or jog. Paths wind through 600-plus acres of forested and wide-open spaces. Minutes into your workout, it's easy to forget you are surrounded by the bustling city, thanks to the beautiful landscape.

Bringing the kiddos with you? Take a detour from the path to enjoy the Sunrise Boundless Playground, an area made up of brightly colored equipment and shaded areas. Better yet, take everyone on the Sedgwick County Art Walk, located near the 13th Street entrance. The limestone path leads visitors to an outdoor exhibit of public art sculptures made by six Kansas artists. Wind through the turtle maze to read the message at the end of the trail or guess the height of the towering totem pole.

6501 W 21st St. N, 316-794-2774
sedgwickcounty.org/parks/sedgwick-county-park

RIDE BIKES
DURING OPEN STREETS ICT

Imagine riding your bike in the street alongside hundreds of others who smile from behind the handlebars. Open Streets ICT, a free event in the fall, temporarily closes Douglas Avenue from the College Hill neighborhood to the Delano District to allow cyclists (and walkers!) to exercise together in the spirit of health and wellness. The spring event centers around the north side's Nomar Market.

Bike culture thrives in Wichita twice a year during Open Streets ICT. Proud parents pull their kids in bike trailers down an open stretch of road. Couples pedal happily on tandems. The occasional bike bell rings out in the distance. When it's time for a break, participants temporarily park their bikes to visit food trucks and watch street performers. Children have their faces painted, play with bubbles, and play in Naftzger Park's splash pad.

openstreetsict.com

BE BLOWN AWAY
BY THE WICHITA WIND SURGE

The crack of the bat. The roar of the crowd. The city's Minor League baseball team Wichita Wind Surge brings fans to their feet at Riverfront Stadium from April to September. If it's baseball season, you should be there to experience high-energy innings as the Surge race to the Double-A Central crown. Whether you cheer on the home team from general seating, the berm (kids love it!), or reserved seating, the energy is palpable.

Take a break from the action to order concessions or a cold one from a nearby beer stand. Hometown favorite, Freddy's Frozen Custard & Steakburgers, is a sure-win. Take time to admire the murals and sculptures inside and outside of Riverfront Stadium—many were created by local artists. Look for Windy, the team's mascot, for a photo opportunity.

275 S McLean Blvd., 316-221-8100
windsurge.com

TIP

Every game promises a good time
because of fun promotions like
Thirsty Thursday, Wind Surge Wednesday,
and Kids Club Game on select Sundays.
Don't miss the end of the season postgame
fireworks, with the city's skyline
as the backdrop.

TRY WATER SPORTS
ON THE ARKANSAS RIVER

One of the best ways to take in the downtown scenery is from a kayak, paddleboard, or pedal boat on the Arkansas River. Boats and Bikes at River Vista, staffed by members of the Wichita State University Shocker Rowing Team, supplies watercraft for rent by the hour with 24-hour notice for reservations.

Open to locals and visitors of all experience levels, the helpful staff guides you through the experience. It's as easy as filling out a waiver and then setting out on the water. The staff provides instructions for using the equipment and launches the boats on the water for you. Some kayakers and paddleboarders like to travel to the the *Keeper of the Plains* or north as far as the river allows before returning to the dock. Visit the website or call ahead to check hours of operation, as they vary depending on the season and weather conditions.

150 N McLean Blvd., B2, 316-265-9359
wichita.edu/boatsandbikes

TIP
For group experiences, ask Boats and Bikes about special events such as kayaking on July 4 to watch the Red, White & Boom! fireworks from the water.

VIEW ANIMALS
AT KANSAS WILDLIFE EXHIBIT

Do you see Odin the owl, Ravioli the hawk, or Pokey the opossum? The Kansas Wildlife Exhibit at Central Riverside Park has wowed animal lovers since 1988 with 25 animal species. The location has been the site of one kind of zoo or another since 1901. In fact, it served as the city's first zoo until the Sedgwick County Zoo opened in 1974.

Families have visited the animal exhibit for decades to get a glimpse at the animals, especially during mealtime. Rufus the bobcat can be entertaining to watch while he works to get to his food inside a box. Čhápa, the beaver, has its own fans for having once escaped the exhibit, only to be seen days later attempting to re-enter its home. Kids are captivated by the box turtles that feed in plain sight. Parents point out hidden creatures to their children. Stay tuned to the Facebook page for indoor exhibit viewing opportunities during noon feeding times.

700 N Nims St., 316-337-9211
facebook.com/kansaswildlifeexhibit

TIP
Kids will love the nearby splash pad and playground during the summer months.

EXPLORE
THE ARKANSAS RIVER TRAIL

The view of the flowing river. The Wichita skyline. Taking a walk or biking via the Arkansas River Trail promises adventure seekers an easy-to-navigate, paved path with great views. Nearly 11 miles in length, it sees light traffic and is open to pet owners with leashed dogs. Although cyclists are known to enjoy the trail, it's also common to see walkers or joggers using it. Downtown residents have easy access to the trail at various entry points in the urban corridor.

Keeper of the Plains is a scenic place to start or end one's excursion. Stopping points along the trail in the downtown area include Museums on the River, Veterans' Memorial Park, Riverside Park, and Sims Park. Need a break? Sit down on a bench and enjoy the scenery during the day or watch a sunset over the river.

Downtown Wichita, 316-268-4361

GET YOUR GAME ON
AT CHICKEN N PICKLE

"Great food, Great friends, Great fun" await at Chicken N Pickle. The indoor/outdoor entertainment complex is like a giant playground for all ages. Feeling competitive? Take out your adrenaline on a pickleball court. There are six indoor courts and four outdoor courts. If laid-back fun is more your speed, take a turn at one of the yard games outdoors like cornhole, life-size Jenga or Connect 4. Good times don't end there. Head inside to find shuffleboard tables and TVs on nearly every wall to watch collegiate or pro teams compete on-screen.

Take a break from the activity and enjoy a fried chicken sandwich from the fast-casual restaurant, also known for Taco Tuesday. Catch Happy Hour at the bar Monday through Friday. Sit upstairs for views from the Boulevard Rooftop patio.

1240 N Greenwich Rd., 316-535-7150
chickennpickle.com/wichita

WALK ON THE WILD SIDE
AT SEDGWICK COUNTY ZOO

Considered one of the best zoos in the Midwest, the Sedgwick County Zoo is touted as the number-one outdoor family tourist attraction in Kansas. It's home to over 3,000 animals and more than 400 different species.

The expansive park represents multiple continents. Watch elephants drink water. Dodge flying birds inside the tropics. Play peekaboo with gorillas and chimpanzees. It's a wild time! Get even closer to the animals by purchasing advance tickets for a Wild Encounter or the Giraffe Feeding Station. Visitors may appreciate seeing the animals from a new perspective via a boat tour or the tram.

5555 W Zoo Blvd., 316-660-9453
scz.org

TIP
If you visit the zoo on a Wednesday from November through February, general admission tickets are only $3 per person.

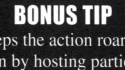

BONUS TIP

The zoo keeps the action roaring after the sun goes down by hosting parties for all ages. Attend popular events like Zoobilee or Creature Campout for the ultimate park adventure.

ROOT FOR A CADDY
AT WICHITA OPEN'S 17TH HOLE

Considered the best ticket on the tour, the Wichita Open is not your average 72-hole golf tournament. The PGA Korn Ferry Tour brings even the most reluctant golf fans to Crestview Country Club every June to enjoy the game, plus a party atmosphere. Attendees can expect prize giveaways, a DJ, and food and drinks during the weeklong event.

An event highlight is sitting on the 17th hole to watch as caddies race to the green while carrying their golfers' bags on their backs. The crowd roars, standing with arms raised. As the caddies cross the green's turf, applause erupts and the event's emcee declares a winner. If you're lucky, the victorious caddy may hand a souvenir to you in the stands.

1000 N 127th St. E, 316-733-1344
wichitaopen.com

BURN OFF ENERGY
AT WICHITA SPORTS FORUM

Be ready to move! Wichita Sports Forum is a multi-sport, extreme air sports complex that provides active individuals a place to let loose and have fun. After signing a waiver and putting on a wristband, you're good to go. Conjure up your inner ninja and maneuver through the obstacles over the foam pit. Test your rock-wall-climbing skills. Wish you were a basketball pro? Practice your moves on the Air Dunk. How high can you bounce? Kids and adults alike love the Flight Zone trampoline. Super Tramps make it easy to polish one's flips, twists, and landings.

If visiting with a group, reserving a basketball or sand volleyball court is the way to go. Serious players can ask about joining a league open to various age groups.

2668 N Greenwich Ct., 316-201-1414
wichitasportsforum.com

STUDY WILDLIFE
AT GREAT PLAINS NATURE CENTER

The Great Plains Nature Center, nestled inside Chisholm Creek Park, offers visitors a chance to learn about the many species that live in the region's prairies and wetlands. Nature lovers of all ages can view animal exhibits, try hands-on exhibits, and study the climate of the Great Plains for free. Birders flock to the Bob Gress Wildlife Observatory to watch feeders in action.

Step outside the center into 282 acres of natural habitat, including four paved walking trails, ranging from 0.5 miles to 1.7 miles. Trail kiosks provide helpful tips. Quiet observers often see turkeys, white-tailed deer, waterfowl, and reptiles under the canopy of trees and across open fields. Anglers appreciate catch-and-release fishing at Island Pond and Chisholm Lake.

6232 E 29th St. N, 316-683-5499
gpnc.org

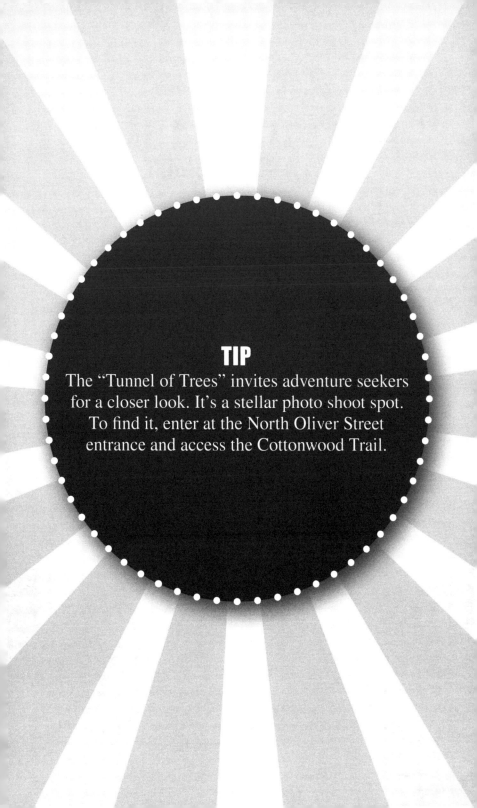

TIP

The "Tunnel of Trees" invites adventure seekers for a closer look. It's a stellar photo shoot spot. To find it, enter at the North Oliver Street entrance and access the Cottonwood Trail.

PERFECT YOUR GAME
ON A GOLF COURSE

"Fore!" Golfers have the option of playing four, 18-hole, public courses within the city limits. Operated by the City of Wichita Park & Recreation Department, the fairways and greens are well-maintained, so golfers of all skill levels can play high-quality courses. If your short game needs a little TLC, finesse it at 5-Hole Pitch & Putt, located at MacDonald Golf Course.

Golfers of all ages and abilities are encouraged to learn the game. Wichita Golf offers lessons for beginners to advanced individuals, including golfers as young as nine years old. Newbies can get hands-on instruction during a free, one-hour clinic.

433 S 135th St., 316-219-9700
840 N Yale Ave., 316-688-9391
1931 S Tyler Rd., 316-337-9494
2020 W Murdock St., 316-337-9100
golfwichita.com

TIP

The free Golf Wichita mobile app allows you to schedule tee times, keep an interactive scorecard, and be notified of course news. It allows you to access GPS on the course without using any of your phone's data.

CULTURE AND HISTORY

PAY TRIBUTE
AT KANSAS FIREFIGHTERS MUSEUM

The heroes who worked as firefighters in Wichita made history at Engine House No. 6. Built in 1906, it was the last horse-drawn station in the city and the first all-mechanized fire department in the United States. Today, the Kansas Firefighters Museum occupies the building that is listed on the National and Kansas registers of historic places.

It's open on Saturdays, and visitors can sit on an antique fire truck, ring a fire bell, and browse two floors of artifacts. Private group tours are available by appointment. The Kansas Fallen Firefighters Memorial south of the museum honors Kansans who died in the line of duty. Pay tribute by reading "A Fireman's Prayer," written by Wichitan A. W. (Smokey) Linn.

1300 S Broadway St., 316-264-5990
kansasfirefightersmuseum.com

TIP
Free parking is available across the street in a dedicated lot, which comes in handy during two popular annual events: the September 11 Remembrance Ceremony and the Kansas Fallen Fighters Memorial in October.

SALUTE A HERO
AT VETERANS' MEMORIAL PARK

Under a shaded canopy of trees stands multiple monuments at Veterans' Memorial Park for those who sacrificed all in their devotion to duty. A total of 18 memorials representing six wars are available to view at no cost. From American Gold Star Mothers to those affected by Vietnam, the memorials are dedicated to people whose lives were changed by war. Symbolic of the nation's patriotism, Flag Pavilion features the evolution of America's flag since its creation.

The park provides a space for quiet reflection and a chance to thank the brave men and women who served in the US military. Federal holidays such as Veterans Day, as well as commemoration ceremonies, are recognized at the park with organized events. A short walk from the city's iconic *Keeper of the Plains*, the park also is accessible by car. Parking is available on the north side of the park.

339 Veterans Pkwy., 316-219-9777
wichitaveteransmemorialpark.com

EXPAND YOUR MIND
AT ULRICH MUSEUM OF ART

Tucked away on the south side of Wichita State University's campus sits Ulrich Museum of Art, a place where visitors connect with modern and contemporary artwork in unexpected ways. Sit in a room and experience sound art. Feel dwarfed by large-scale paintings. Maze through three-dimensional artwork.

Since 1974, the museum has celebrated artists' work in its permanent collection and rotating exhibition galleries. The museum extends its showcase outdoors to the Martin H. Bush Outdoor Sculpture Collection, featuring over 80 works spread across the university's campus. Use the museum's mobile app to locate notable works like *Twister Grande* by Alice Aycock or *Millipede* by Tom Otterness.

The museum welcomes art enthusiasts indoors six days a week. Admission is always free. Guided, in-gallery tour requests must be submitted a month in advance.

1845 Fairmount St., 316-978-3664
ulrich.wichita.edu

STEP BACK IN TIME
AT OLD COWTOWN MUSEUM

Have you ever wondered what it would have been like to live in Wichita during the days of cattle drives and the Chisholm Trail? Cowboys, early settlers, and main street shops set the scene at Old Cowtown Museum.

Follow the dirt road into an old residential street, complete with 50 historic and recreated buildings. Witness gunfights on Main Street six days a week, or learn about pioneer frontier life in the late 1860s from costumed interpreters. Visit Cowtown at dusk for a ghost tour during First Friday Late Nights!. Experiencing Cowtown under the stars transports you to another place in time. Never miss a moment of fun—check the museum's calendar for updated seasonal events. Steampunk Weekend, Boos and Brews, and the patriotic party Celebrate America!, are crowd-pleasers.

1865 W Museum Blvd., 316-219-1871
oldcowtown.org

TIP
Dedicate at least two hours to tour the building, take a wagon ride, and listen to interpreters. Don't forget to buy old-time candy in the gift shop.

HONE IN ON HERITAGE
AT WICHITA-SEDGWICK COUNTY HISTORICAL MUSEUM

If the Wichita-Sedgwick County Historical Museum's goal is to provide a world-class experience that tells the story of the people and places who made the region great, they've succeeded. Completed in 1892 as Wichita's first city hall, the building was considered the "Palace of the Plains." Now, it displays permanent and special collections, featuring over 80,000 artifacts from 1865 to the present day.

The museum is four floors of well-designed spaces. Step into "A Child's World" to imagine a time of one-room schoolhouses. Tour "A Wichita Cottage" to see an interpretation of what a middle-class home looked like in 1890. Learn about the heritage of the Wichita Indians who gave the city its name, the days of booming downtown businesses, and the rise of The Air Capital of the World.

204 S Main St., 316-265-9314
wichitahistory.org

TIP

Museum admission grants access to nearby Heritage Square Park, a serene courtyard featuring beautiful landscaping and a gazebo. Bring your lunch and enjoy concerts in the courtyard on Wednesdays at noon during September.

CONTEMPLATE THE COLLECTIONS
AT MUSEUM OF WORLD TREASURES

"How did they get so many unique artifacts under one roof?" is something you might think as you make your way through the Museum of World Treasures. Devoting at least two hours to peruse three floors of permanent collections is best.

Interested in natural history? Skeletons like Ivan the Tyrannosaurus rex anchor the first-floor Fossil Gallery. Curious about life during the time of war? The second floor tells the story of times of conflict dating to the Civil War. If studying world civilizations excites you, you'll appreciate collections including authentic shrunken heads, mummies, and Roman coins.

Kids can't get enough, so Midnight at the Museum Camp-Ins keep the learning fun. Plus, they sleep among dinosaurs! Events designed for adults like Senior Wednesday and Coffee with the Curator are enriching activities.

835 E 1st St., 316-263-1311
worldtreasures.org

WIND YOUR WAY
THROUGH WICHITA ART MUSEUM

As you follow your path through the Wichita Art Museum, you quickly realize that you're standing among the greats. Edward Hopper. Mary Cassatt. Dale Chihuly. Each artist is part of a massive collection of American art housed under one roof. On-loan exhibits also showcase top-notch artwork.

The museum is a place for everyone to enjoy, a family-friendly setting where kids appreciate a room dedicated to them with opportunities to create artwork. And that's just what's inside the museum. A self-guided sculpture tour awaits visitors who exit the museum's doors to the Art Garden. Walk the pathways to discover sculptures like Tom Otterness's *Dreamers Awake*, which is an 8 Wonders of Kansas art finalist.

1400 W Museum Blvd., 316-268-4921
wichitaartmuseum.org

TIP

Docent-led tours are available to groups if booked in advance.
The museum hosts drop-in tours of the impressive outdoor sculpture collection. Check the website for details.

IMMERSE YOURSELF IN NATIVE AMERICAN CULTURE
AT MID-AMERICA ALL-INDIAN MUSEUM

A top attraction in the city, Mid-America All-Indian Museum draws individuals who want to learn more about Native American culture and art. Open to all ages, its interactive displays incorporate hands-on exhibits, videos, and artifacts.

The indoor gallery showcases paintings and sketches from Blackbear Bosin, the artist who created the *Keeper of the Plains* statue located on the river, steps from the museum. The Gallery of Nations exhibits colorful flags representing Wichita tribes, and an artfully crafted totem pole. Visitors can learn the history of powwow dances and how they are performed from a nearby photography exhibit.

Notable annual events such as the Trail of Tears Memorial, Back to School Powwow, and the Indian Art Market will leave you with a deeper understanding of Native American culture.

650 N Seneca St., 316-350-3340
theindiancenter.org

FOSTER YOUR CREATIVITY
AT MARK ARTS

Mark Arts offers one-night, introductory workshops that teach individuals to foster their creativity and stretch the bounds of artistry. The center, which also doubles as an art gallery, hosts a long list of classes that don't require experience or supplies. Instructors teach students mediums from painting to printmaking inside the School of Creativity Gallery or the Gladys and Karl T. Wiedemann Gallery.

Feeling fabulous about your new skills? Celebration is in order. Adult students are allowed to bring a beverage of choice to class—Mark Arts supplies the glasses. If taking a single session ignites your interest, there are a variety of workshops available to further expand your creativity. Why not take a class in the culinary arts or jewelry making? Enroll and enjoy the journey.

1307 N Rock Rd., 316-634-2787
markartsks.com

PUTT-PUTT
TO THE PIZZA HUT MUSEUM

Do you have fond memories of the Pizza Hut Book-It™ program? A self-guided tour of the Home of the Hut, the original restaurant's building, is a welcomed blast from the past. Wichita is proud of the pizza chain's hometown legacy, launched by college students, the Carney brothers, in 1958.

Visitors are encouraged to interact with the Tactile Library and take a selfie with the restaurant chain's original mascot, Pizza Pete. The museum serves up a hand-selected collection of memorabilia, from branded basketball shoes to pizza-themed children's toys. Pizza Hut lovers rejoice! The museum is free to visit and open to the public.

2090 Innovation Blvd., 316-978-4488
wichita.edu/museums/pizzahutmuseum

TIP
The original sauce recipe was written on a napkin. What is your favorite Pizza Hut memory? Sit down at the table, write it on a napkin, and post it on the Reflections Board.

SHOUT "ALL ABOARD!"
AT GREAT PLAINS
TRANSPORTATION MUSEUM

Since its doors opened in 1986, the Great Plains Transportation Museum has given train enthusiasts a chance to get close to steam locomotives, meticulously restored train cars, and railroad equipment. Railroad fans have access to historic prints, tools, and railroad artifacts in the museum's one-room exhibit. Curious about Wichita's railroad heritage and Union Station? Ask the friendly, knowledgeable staff.

Two industrial locomotives, a tank car, and a diesel-electric locomotive are just some of the rail cars on display. At this family-friendly destination, kids love climbing inside the wooden caboose—a perfect photo opportunity. Don't put the brakes on the fun just yet. The gift shop gives railway buffs a chance to stock up on merchandise before they go home. Journey into the past during Railfest, the first two weekends in October.

700 E Douglas Ave., 316-263-0944
gptm.us

APPRECIATE ARCHITECTURE
AT FRANK LLOYD WRIGHT'S ALLEN HOUSE

During the early years of the College Hill neighborhood, Henry J. Allen and his wife commissioned famous architect Frank Lloyd Wright in 1915 to design their home to later be built there. Every detail of the house, from its structural design to the handcrafted furniture, reflects Wright's style.

An example of the architect's Prairie Style, Allen House is designed horizontally to mimic the Midwest's landscape. Its massive living room and dining room partially frame an outdoor garden and koi pond. Every effort was made to create continuity between the indoors and the outdoors, from the oversized, stained-glass windows to the woodwork. To see Allen House, which he referred to as "among my best," sign up for a tour Wednesday through Sunday or attend a special event.

255 N Roosevelt St., 316-687-1027
flwrightwichita.org

ADMIRE
THE AWE-INSPIRING
KEEPER OF THE PLAINS

The city was named for the Wichita tribe at the insistence of one of its founders, J. R. Mead. To fully understand the impact of Native American culture, a visit to the iconic *Keeper of the Plains* statue is a must-see destination. It is a sight to behold.

Standing proudly at the confluence of the Big and Little Arkansas rivers since 1974, the 44-foot COR-TEN® steel statue designed by Blackbear Bosin is an awe-inspiring symbol for the city. At the plaza, listen closely to hear the sounds of Native American chants while reading about symbols. Return at 7 p.m. (fall and winter) or 9 p.m. (spring and summer) to see the *Keeper of the Plains* shining brightly from the "Ring of Fire" at its base. The area is open to the public year-round and is free to enjoy.

339 Veterans Pkwy., 316-268-4497
wichita.gov/arts/pages/keeper.aspx

TIP
Stop by the nearby Mid-America All-Indian Museum to learn more about the *Keeper of the Plains* artist Blackbear Bosin. The museum's gift store is an ideal place to shop for Wichita-themed items featuring the statue.

GEEK OUT ON PLANES
AT THE KANSAS AVIATION MUSEUM

Wichita's original municipal airport was one of the busiest airports in the nation after its completion in 1935. A halfway point across the county, the airfield brought some of the nation's most famous celebrities to "The Air Capital of the World." Today, it is a museum providing visitors an opportunity to journey through Kansas's great aviation past.

The indoor exhibits focus on aspects of aviation, from the impact of the city's manufacturing industry to the logistics of flight. The journey through history continues with a collection of restored aircraft, including a 1920 Laird Swallowtail, 1932 Beechcraft Model 17 Staggerwing, and the actual 1929 Travel Air D4000 flown by Wichitan Louise Thaden in the Powder Puff Derby. Walk outdoors to get a closer look at retired aircraft.

3350 S George Washington Blvd., 316-683-9242
kansasaviationmuseum.org

TIP
Climb the stairs to the control tower for a 360-degree, bird's-eye view of the city. Listen to live Air Traffic Control broadcasts for an immersive experience.

HONOR LEGACY
AT KANSAS AFRICAN AMERICAN MUSEUM

The Kansas African American Museum's building and its contents are rich in history. Formerly the Calvary Baptist Church, it was built in 1917 and relocated to its current location in 1972. Now, it's open as a museum that honors the experience of African Americans and their legacy.

Visitors can expect to find storytelling exhibits on the first floor, which are updated every three months. Past exhibits have included writer and photographer Gordon Parks's work, the traveling show "Sorting Out Race," and "Bring it On Blues," among others. A permanent collection, "Africa to Kansas," showcases artifacts on the first floor. A short walk upstairs to the "Journey Through Kansas" exhibit gives museumgoers a better understanding of the people and places that affected the African American community.

601 N Water St., 316-262-7651
tkaamuseum.org

TIP
Metered street parking is limited near the museum. Park inside the parking garage across the street, and a museum employee will validate your parking.

CLIMB INTO THE BELLY OF A WARBIRD
AT B-29 DOC HANGAR, EDUCATION AND VISITORS CENTER

Rivet guns buzzed. Workers scrambled. The year was 1944 and the production of World War II warbirds was at its height when Doc, a B-29 Superfortress, rolled off the assembly line at Boeing with one mission—to defeat Japan. The Wichita Boeing Company built 1,644 B-29s.

Doc was a technological marvel of the early 1940s. After its duties came to an end, Doc sat in the Mojave Desert for over four decades. The story didn't end there. Tony Mazzolini rescued Doc and returned it to Wichita, where volunteers spent over 16 years (450,000 hours) restoring it to pristine condition. Today, it flies as a living museum across the country to air shows and makes tour stops. It flies about 100 hours every year. When not in the air, it rests in a private hangar where visitors can see it up-close.

1788 S Airport Rd., 316-260-4312
b29doc.com

TIP

You can climb the ladder into the belly of Doc for an additional fee. Volunteers are happy to answer questions about plane mechanics. Get a look inside the hangar by viewing a live webcam via the website.

SHOPPING AND FASHION

SHOP FOR A NEW READ
AT WATERMARK BOOKS & CAFÉ

Independent bookstores are incredibly cool, and no one does it better than Watermark Books & Café. Let the journey to discover a new read begin. The shelves are stocked with select, highly coveted books that keep avid readers wanting more. If you don't find the read you're looking for, the staff will bend over backward to find and order it for you. Seasoned readers have the option of joining the frequent buyer program.

The place is typically abuzz with activity. Regular book signing events featuring Midwest authors generate lines of patrons. The cafe prepares scratch-made meals and baked goods for carryout. The reach-in refrigerator is stocked with containers of salads and soups for shoppers on the go.

4701 E Douglas Ave., 316-682-1181
watermarkbooks.com

TIP

The bookstore often has signed books in stock. Ask about joining the Signed First Editions Club for exclusive access to collectors' titles. Register for the Seasoned Readers frequent buyer program. For every $100 you spend in either the bookstore or café, you will receive a $10 certificate to be redeemed on a future purchase.

BUY GRILLING SUPPLIES
AT ALL THINGS BARBECUE

It's hard to resist buying BBQ seasoning, hot sauce, or marinade once you step inside All Things Barbecue. Maybe it's because you're surrounded by pellet smokers and grills. Perhaps it's because Chef Tom is known to offer shoppers tasty food samples Monday through Friday if he's testing recipes. Either way, you're bound to purchase something from brines to burger presses.

Don't let the size of the Yoder smokers on the showroom floor intimidate you. The friendly and knowledgeable staff welcomes questions from backyard barbecuers of all skill sets. Questioning how to use a smoke box? Unsure of which knife set to buy? They love to talk shop. The knowledge sharing doesn't stop there. Chef Tom has a massive following on the shop's YouTube channel. Barbecue fans check in twice a week to view new recipe tutorials.

818 W Douglas Ave., 316-440-3950
atbbq.com

SPEND MONEY ON OTHERS
AT BEST OF TIMES CARDS & GIFTS

Is there a person in your life who is hard to buy for? Best of Times Cards & Gifts is the place to shop. Owner Nancy Robinson has stocked the store with fabulous gifts and unique greeting cards since 1981. If you don't walk out of the store with the perfect gift for someone, you are not looking hard enough.

The locally owned shop is as unique as the products it carries. From comical socks and quirky collectibles to handbags to hard candy, you'll find it there. Shoppers also will appreciate the store's large selection of seasonal decor and gifts. Need a present for a baby shower or birthday party, or perhaps a hostess gift? Show someone you care by filling a gift bag with items that suit their personality.

6452 E Central Ave., 316-634-3805
bestoftimesgifts.com

SHOP AND DINE LOCAL
AT CLIFTON SQUARE

Unlike a mall, Clifton Square is a mini shopping district for those who prefer to spend their dollars locally. Two-story houses converted into small businesses have invited visitors to shop the square since 1972.

For many east siders, Clifton Square has served as a place where childhood memories were made. Kids often walk over after school to buy ice cream. Parents meet friends for Happy Hour at restaurants. For those looking for a place to relax and unwind, Clifton Square is home to unhurried boutique shopping, salons, and a tearoom. Lovers of art will adore the square for its colorful murals. Walk the brick sidewalks that weave throughout the square to get a glimpse of street art painted by local artists.

3700 E Douglas Ave., 316-371-9209
facebook.com/cliftonsquarewichita

TIP
Sit back and relax inside the gazebo. It offers a great vantage point of the shopping district.

PURCHASE
ICT FLAG SWAG
AT THE WORKROOM

The Workroom is Wichita's go-to store to shop for ICT flag swag. The store is the hub for all things Wichita-centric and carries what is considered to be the largest inventory of ICT flag swag in the city. Wichitans know the letters ICT are the airport's call letters for the city. A resurgence of enthusiasm for Wichita has grown since the introduction of the city's flag. Shoppers who want to show their Wichita pride can buy everything from apparel to artwork at the boutique.

Store owner Janelle King is an advocate for the arts and supporting local. The Workroom's retail inventory largely consists of items made by local creators. The shop hosts the second Saturday artisan market showcasing vendors, food trucks, and live music for all ages to enjoy. Check the store's Facebook page for upcoming events like Final Friday.

150 N Cleveland Ave., 316-295-4520
theworkroomict.com

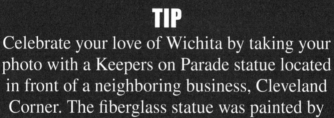

TIP

Celebrate your love of Wichita by taking your photo with a Keepers on Parade statue located in front of a neighboring business, Cleveland Corner. The fiberglass statue was painted by Aaron Jackson Bowman.

GET FITTED
AT HATMAN JACK'S
WICHITA HAT WORKS

One of the longest-running small businesses in the city, Hatman Jack's Wichita Hat Works has helped hat lovers look their best for decades. Fashion-forward shoppers can have customized hats tailored to perfection to suit their style. Need a hat for a special occasion or everyday wear? The third-largest hat shop in the country carries them.

Shoppers to the store, located in the historic Delano District, can select from hats on display and have them modified to suit their needs while they wait. Hats off to owner Jack Kellogg, who does custom fittings for customers to ensure quality construction. The store attracts repeat customers who often bring friends and family members to the shop. It is a must-visit travel destination in the city.

601 W Douglas Ave., 316-264-4881
hatmanjacks.com

GEAR UP
FOR GROWING SEASON
AT HILLSIDE FEED & SEED

Shopping at Hillside Feed & Seed is a gardener's delight. A hidden gem, the shop sells everything a gardener needs, year-round. You're invited to "embrace your inner plant nerd" when shopping for botanicals. The vegetable and flowering plants are always full and healthy. Shop the garden-ready selection of fruit-producing plants. Need pots, gloves, or bug spray? They've got it all.

Green thumbs and newbie gardeners will drool over the store's vast inventory of flower and vegetable seed packets. In a nearby room, backyard birders can stock up on bulk seed sold by the pound. The bins are filled with sunflower seed, thistle, millet, peanuts, and cracked corn. Don't forget to treat yourself, too. Grab a jar of fresh salsa or Kansas-made honey on your way to the register.

1805 S Hillside St., 316-685-7361
hillsidefeed.com

SUPPORT SMALL BUSINESS
AT REVOLUTSIA

What is more unique than shopping at a shipping container mall? Revolutsia's retail stores, restaurants, and independently owned businesses enclose a courtyard where locals and visitors appreciate a sense of community.

It's one-stop shopping for everything from haircuts and Hispanic artisan gifts to soaps and sweet treats. You can wrestle through racks for vintage clothes. Perfect your productivity by buying planners and pens. Revolutsia's retail stores sell a little bit of everything. If you fancy a bite to eat or something to sip on, spend time in Fleur de Vin, Prost, Better Yet Coffee, or Taco Locale. Order food to go from Boards, Monica's Bundt Cake, or shop Ze German Markt.

2721 E Central Ave., 316-290-9596
revolutsia.com

TIP

Send cheers with a stein in hand at Prost's Oktoberfest party, held every September in the restaurant's biergarten. Live folk music, imported beer, and bratwursts make for a celebratory setting.

GO GOURMET
AT KERNEL'S POPCORN EXPRESS

Nothing is harder to resist during a snack attack than a fresh batch of gourmet popcorn. Kernel's Popcorn Express carries over 30 handcrafted flavors, including seasonal varieties prepared on site. It's the place to shop for delicious popcorn when you feel a craving coming on. You'll find it hard to leave the store with only one bag of popcorn in hand. Popular flavors like Tutti Fruitti, Bacon Cheddar, and Praline Pecan keep die-hard fans coming back for more. The store's candy and popcorn combinations, like the ever-popular Zombie Korn at Halloween time, are irresistible.

Why buy a single bag of popcorn? Purchase a signature flavor box or create your own popcorn tin, which makes a thoughtful, customized gift. Or perhaps you could stash a bag or two in your desk drawer at work. Either way, it won't last long.

1101 E 2nd St. N, 316-263-6886
kernelspopcornexpress.com

FIND A LAST-MINUTE GIFT
AT LUCINDA'S

A few minutes into shopping at Lucinda's in Old Town, you know your wallet is in trouble. It's the kind of boutique where you're bound to find a present for someone and a few more for yourself. From chic clothing to goofy gifts, they carry it—much of it made by local artisans and small business owners. Voted Best Gift Shop by *Wichita Eagle* readers, Lucinda's has been making shoppers happy for over 20 years with a "quirky mix of clever things."

Do you know someone who would love a pair of silly socks or comical drink coasters? They make great party gifts. For the person in your life who wears their Kansas pride on their sleeve, they stock sunflower and Wichita-themed merchandise. Women love their clothing inventory. It's as simple as adding a humorous greeting card, and you are a gift-giving hero.

329 N Mead St., 316-264-1080
lucindas.net

GIVE IN
TO YOUR CRAVINGS
AT NIFTY NUT HOUSE

Anyone with a sweet tooth or salt craving will tell you that the best place to stock up on snacks is the Nifty Nut House. The store is run by third-generation family members, supplying shoppers with a wide selection of nuts, dried fruits, gummies, and nostalgic candy.

Grab a basket to fill up with a heap of goodies. The smell of flavorful snacks will draw you to the center section of the store, where friendly employees stand ready to weigh Sesame Party Mix, Corn Nuggets, and nuts by the pound. A fan of retro sweets? They carry everything from Swedish Fish to Black Jack chewing gum. A trip to this well-loved destination is an experience. Take a group picture from the wooden photo booth board near the entrance, a fun option for families. Oh, and good luck making it to the car without opening your bag of treats.

537 N St. Francis St., 316-265-0571
niftynuthouse.com

CONNECT WITH THE COMMUNITY
AT OLD TOWN FARM & ART MARKET

You show up to shop for farm-fresh produce, flowers, and handmade gifts. You leave, having made new friends. The Old Town Farm & Art Market is a central gathering place for people every Saturday from April to October and November to December in downtown Wichita. Everyone is welcome. The place stirs with parents pushing strollers, dogs on leashes, and shoppers visiting vendors' tents. The smell of freshly grilled food forms long lines from booths, and coffee lovers wait at the espresso truck. Live music on the north side of the square inspires visitors to dance.

The market has introduced people to one another for over 30 years. People come together in the spirit of shopping and supporting local at the market. The sense of community is the feeling that keeps them coming back.

835 E 1st St. N, 316-337-5770
oldtownfarmandartmarket.com

WAKE UP
AND SMELL THE COFFEE
AT THE SPICE MERCHANT

One step inside The Spice Merchant, and the coffee aroma hits you. Since 1985, the shop has roasted globally sourced coffee beans for shoppers who want a premium cup of joe at home. Not sure which coffee to buy? Ask the roasters for a sample of the day.

A home chef's paradise, the store can be counted on to carry spices you need as well as exotic ones you didn't know you needed, like Vietnamese cinnamon and hickory smoke powder. You can purchase as much or as little of them as you want. Specialty foods, kitchen gadgets, loose-leaf tea, and amusing gifts keep people returning to stock up on their favorites. As you make your way through the store's cozy aisles, you're guaranteed to purchase more than you expected to buy. Chocolate truffles or hard candy, anyone?

1300 E Douglas Ave., 316-263-4121
spicemerchant.com

SHOP FOR SUSTAINABLE PRODUCTS
AT GRATE FILL

For every person who strives to live a sustainable lifestyle, Grate Fill is the answer. The refill shop stocks non-toxic, eco-friendly home and hygiene products. A first of its kind in Wichita, it resembles a store you would find in a larger city.

Shoppers can bring in reusable bottles or purchase them at the store to fill with a plethora of products, ranging from laundry soap to shampoo and conditioner. Store staff bases the price of purchase on the ounces filled. Bath supplies like bamboo toothbrushes, cleansing sponges, and natural toothpaste line the shelves. Tables are covered in all-natural makeup, jewelry, and locally made artisan gifts. If living a zero-waste lifestyle is your mission, swap your plastic bag for a Grate Fill canvas tote and start shopping.

2000 N Rock Rd. Suite 122, 316-352-7476
gratefill.com

ACTIVITIES
BY SEASON

WINTER

Start Your Day at Reverie Roasters, 34

Enjoy a Slice of Heaven at Peace Love & Pie, 2

Become a Fan of Music Theatre of Wichita, 57

Lace Up Your Skates at Wichita Ice Center, 74

Shop for a New Read at Watermark Books & Café, 116

Lick the Bowl Clean at Tanya's Soup Kitchen, 6

Get Fitted at Hatman Jack's Wichita Hat Works, 122

SPRING

Choose Dinner with a View at Newport Grill, 10

Celebrate St. Patrick's Day at the Artichoke Sandwichbar, 55

Be Blown Away by the Wichita Wind Surge, 80

Gaze at the Gardens at Botanica, 44

Perfect Your Game on a Golf Course, 92

Gear Up for Growing Season at Hillside Feed & Seed, 123

Take to the Trails at Sedgwick County Park, 78

SUMMER

FALL

• •

SUGGESTED
ITINERARIES

WICHITA WONDERS

MUSIC LOVERS' MUST-STOPS

FOODIE FAVORITES

HISTORY HOUNDS

OUTDOOR ENTHUSIASTS

SHOP 'TIL YOU DROP

ART AFICIONADOS

ESPECIALLY SPORTS

DATE NIGHT

KID AT HEART

INDEX

• •

• •

· ·